Great Lakes Cold Case Files
Unsolved Murders Of The Great Lakes Region

Wayne Louis Kadar

Avery Color Studios, Inc.
Gwinn, Michigan

© 2013 Avery Color Studios, Inc.

ISBN: 978-1-892384-65-2

Library of Congress Control Number: 2012945822

First Edition 2013

10   9   8   7   6   5   4   3

Published by Avery Color Studios, Inc.
Gwinn, Michigan 49841

Table of Contents

Dedication

As one progresses along the path of life, friends drift in and out, but family is the constant. I am proud to dedicate this book to my wife Karen, our children and their spouses; Brandon and Stacey, Kasie and Chris, and Grant and Kelsey, and to our grandchildren; Dylan, Ariel, Audrey, Cora, Elyse, Benny and Khloe.

Introduction

· ·

Unsolved murders exist in all of the United States and Canadian Provinces. This book concentrates specifically on crimes that have occurred in Michigan, Illinois, Ohio, Indiana, Wisconsin, Pennsylvania, Minnesota and the Canadian Province of Ontario that make up the Great Lakes Region.

The majority of people watch television police shows and see that crimes are solved, most within an hour, and our concept of crime statistics are skewed. We hear that there is no such thing as a perfect crime, but the facts indicate nearly forty percent of all murders nationwide go unsolved each year. The murderers might not have committed a perfect crime but nearly half of them go cold for lack of conviction.

The 2008 Scripps Howard News Service study of the FBI's Uniform Crime Report developed information on homicides for each of the United States for a period from 1980 to 2008. For the purpose of this book the results for the Great Lakes States are presented.

State	Number of Murders	Number Unsolved
Illinois	25,254	8,974
Indiana	9,485	4,098
Michigan	23,682	11,367
Minnesota	3,411	1,358
Ohio	15,831	5,501
Wisconsin	5,051	965

Note: The numbers for Illinois are estimated due to their method of recording data.

While these numbers are disturbing, they have improved since the 1960s when almost 90 percent of homicides were not solved. Improvements in forensic technology and investigative procedures have resulted in bringing more criminals to justice.

The numbers are scary but the number of unsolved murders also reflect lives lost and unfulfilled dreams. Parents, spouses, siblings, and friends grieve for the unnecessary loss of a loved one and are relegated to live a life of questioning what happened? Who did it? Is the perpetrator still within their circle of friends? They wonder if their loved one suffered?

The chapters of this book represent just a few of the many unsolved homicides which have occurred over the years in the Great Lakes region. Some may sound familiar from the intense publicity they generated while others barely earned a mention in the local newspaper. But all left a void in someone else's heart.

All of the chapters of the book are about murders that have gone cold or are still active investigations awaiting information to lead investigators down a new path. All of the chapters need the help of people just like you to come forward and provide leads, no matter how seemingly insignificant, to help bring the murderer to justice.

If anyone has anything that might help out, they are requested to contact their police department, sheriff's department, or state police.

I Am A Cheat But Not A Murderer

Highway M-119 is a scenic drive that curves along the Lake Michigan coast in the northwest corner of the Michigan's lower peninsula. The drive provides vistas of the deep blue waters of the lake and on a clear day Beaver Island can be seen on the horizon. The area is covered in thick, green, densely wooded old growth forests and dotted with historic resorts, homes and cabins.

The area's original inhabitants were the Native Americans of the Ottawa Tribe. They paddled canoes along the bluffs lining the shore between their camps located at present day Harbor Springs twenty miles north to Cross Village. Midway between the two locations a camp was established near a large "crooked tree," a landmark easily visible from the water. In the early 1800s the crooked tree encampment was named after a chief's brother whose Ottawa name was interpreted as "Good Heart."

Through the years the "E" was lost and the name evolved to the present day town of Good Hart, Michigan.

Good Hart is about twenty miles from the Mackinac Bridge that connects the state's upper and lower peninsulas. Throughout the years, the area has needed to adapt to changes. It once relied on fishing and logging

3

as its main source of employment but when the wealthy of Chicago and Detroit discovered the beauty of Northwest Michigan, the area became dependent on tourism.

Good Hart and the surrounding area became a playground for the wealthy, a rural area where the captains of industry and finance could get away from the stress of their daily existence and take pleasure in the tranquility and serene peacefulness of the forests, the sport fishing provided on Lake Michigan, or fishing the small inland lakes, rivers and streams.

One of the few stores along the highway was the Good Hart General Store. The General Store fit its surroundings perfectly, the glass front counters displaying fresh baked goods and the antique National Cash Register ringing up the sales emphasized the store's backwoods charm, endearing it to the affluent cottage crowd.

A local builder and developer, Chauncey Bliss and his son Chauncey Jr., known as "Monnie," built several cottages in the area in the 1950s. Their cottages were distinctive in that they were built with a fieldstone foundation exposed a few feet above ground level and topped with a framework of varnished logs. Many of the Bliss cottages, as they became known, still exist in the area.

One of the Bliss cottages, located about two miles north of Good Hart at the dead end on Lamkin Drive, was purchased by the wealthy Detroit area resident Richard Robison. The Robison family named the cottage "Summerset."

The Robison family had the lakeside cottage built in 1958, the year the oldest child, Richard Jr. was nine years old and the other children, Gary and Randy were 7 and 2 respectively and daughter Susan was yet to be born. It was said that for a cottage in the woods, the Robison's Summerset was quite plush.

The Robison children spent the summers playing on the sandy beach, swimming in Lake Michigan, fishing and exploring the woods. It was their second home; a home where they didn't go to school, didn't have homework to do, they only had to play. "Summerset" was one of their favorite places on earth.

Richard enjoyed the seclusion the cottage offered. Their nearest neighbor, Mrs. Russell Moore, was more that a half mile away.

Mr. Robison was the owner of a Detroit advertising company, a commercial artist and the publisher of the arts magazine, *Impresario*.

In 1968 the Robison family was going to spend most of the summer at the cottage, which was not unusual for the family. The younger kids were on summer break from Lathrup Village Schools, a northwest Detroit suburb,

The Robinson family. Front row, Shirley, Susan and Richard. Back row, Gary, Randy and Richard Jr.

and Richard Jr. was on break from Eastern Michigan University, in Ypsilanti, Michigan.

While relaxing at the cottage Richard Jr. and his father discussed current events, such as America's involvement in the war in Vietnam, which in 1968 was escalating, and the co-ed murders that were haunting both the Eastern Michigan University and the University of Michigan campuses during the 1968 school year. The murder cases occupied the front pages of most of Michigan newspapers. John Norman Collins, a student at Eastern Michigan University was later convicted of one of the murders and connected to several others.

Mr. Robison left the business in the hands of his partner, Joseph Scolaro. The two executives were only a phone call apart and they communicated regularly.

The family arrived at "Summerset" on June 16, 1968.

Forty-two year old Richard Robison told neighbors that the family would be away from "Summerset" for a little while. He said he had chartered an airplane to fly the family from Pellston Airport to Kentucky for business. Then they would fly to Florida to purchase a condominium. Plans then called for the family to return to their vacation home outside of Good Hart.

The day before they were to fly out Richard paid a visit to the home of his cottage caretaker, Monnie Bliss. The Bliss's seventeen-year-old son, Norman, a friend with the Robison teens had been killed, just two days earlier, in a motorcycle accident.

Richard expressed his condolences to Mrs. Bliss and gave her $20.00 asking her to purchase flowers for the funeral. Mr. Robison explained that business was taking the family out of town and they were not able attend the funeral.

While the Robison family was away from their cottage in Good Hart, the tranquil life of Northern Michigan continued for summer visitors and residents alike; children swam and built sand castles on the beach and fishermen hooked their dinner, but that would soon change.

Mrs. Moore, the closest neighbor to the Robison's cottage, began to notice a pungent odor, the stench of death, coming from the direction of the woods near "Summerset." Assuming an animal had died in the woods she disregarded it, but the odor continued to get stronger.

Possibly she thought, an animal had gotten into her neighbor's cottage and died, which was not all that unusual in the woods. Animals attracted by food in the cottage would find an opening, get in, and then not be able to find its way out. Sometimes deer jumped through plate glass windows and became trapped in cottages. The decomposing remains of bats, mice, chipmunks, raccoons, and squirrels were sometimes found in the closed cottages.

Fearing an animal had died in the cottage, Mrs. Moore called Monnie Bliss, the Robison's caretaker, to check it out.

On Monday, July 22, 1968, Monnie and a helper drove to the Robison cottage on Lamkin Drive thinking an animal of the forest had found its way into the crawl space of the cottage and died.

Monnie noticed a handwritten note on the front door that read; *"Be back 7-10. – Robison."* The curtains were pulled closed and the door locked. Monnie walked around the house smelling the odor of death and noticed bullet holes in a window. Bullet holes were not a unusual occurrence in a wooded area known for good hunting, the occasional stray shot sometimes struck a building.

All the doors were locked so Monnie used his key to the cottage and entered.

The stench definitely originated from the cottage. As soon as he opened the door Monnie was met by a burst of air heated to over 80 degrees, the sound of thousands of flies and the un-mistakable odor of death.

He looked to his left and saw the maggot-covered, bloated body of Mrs. Robison lying on the floor. Monnie ran out of the cottage and called the Sheriff's Department.

The deputies and county prosecutor who responded were overcome by the terrible stench in the cottage. The sheriff's deputies needed to wear respirators as they searched the rest of the building and found more bodies.

They found the body of Richard Robison lying on top of a furnace floor register in the hallway. 12-year-old Randy was placed on top of his father and was partially covered with a lavender colored rug.

Eight-year-old Susan's body had been dragged into the hallway and laid close to her father and brother. In the bedroom the bodies of 19-year-old Richard Jr. and 17-year-old Gary lie on the floor apparently where they had been shot and dropped.

Shirley Robison, wife and mother, laid on the living room floor, a plaid blanket covering most of her body. Her pants and underwear had been pulled off and her body was arranged, knees raised and legs spread giving the appearance that she had been sexually assaulted.

The entire Robison family, all six of them had been murdered.

The Emmet County Sheriff's Department called for the Michigan State Police's mobile crime unit to assist with the investigation.

The investigators poured over the grizzly scene searching for any clue that would help them understand the motive for such a heinous crime and evidence to incriminate the murderer or murderers.

The dead bodies had been lying in the house, windows closed with the heat turned up, under the hot July sun for 27 days. The corpses of the entire Robison family were in an advanced state of decomposition, flies had been attracted by the pungent odor and fly larvae were feeding on the bloated corpses.

The forensic investigators pieced together the events that resulted in the death of the Robison family; the killer or killers crept out of the woods up to a window next to the front door. Several shots were fired into the room from a rifle striking Richard Robison in the chest as he sat in a chair. The killer(s) burst through the door turning the rifle on Randy and Shirley and firing on them.

Susan tried to run for cover when the killer(s) shot her. The older boys had been playing cards at a table and ran for the bedroom, presumably to get the rifle stored in the closet. They were gunned down as they ran.

7

Each of the victims was then methodically shot in the head with a .25-caliber handgun. The sadistic murderer(s) took a claw hammer to Susan and bludgeoned her head, leaving the bloody hammer near the body.

The body of Mr. Robison was dragged into the hallway and laid across the hot air furnace floor register. Randy and Susan's bodies were also moved from the living room into the hallway.

The corpses of the two older boys were left in the bedroom and the body of Mrs. Robison was left in the living room with a blanket haphazardly tossed over her lifeless body.

The perpetrator closed all the curtains and turned up the heat as he/she closed up the cottage. A piece of cardboard covered the window that was shot out by the initial assault and a handwritten note was taped to the door.

Residents of neighboring cottages were questioned. The deputies wanted to know when they last saw the Robison family? Had they heard anything out of the ordinary? Had they seen anyone around the Robison cottage?

The owner of the closest cottage was not there at the time of the murders and was not able to offer anything. Living a bit away, a couple remembered hearing gunshots and two men and a woman yelling. But they suspected someone was shooting at seagulls down the beach and didn't go to inquire about the shots.

The first path the investigation took was that of a murder-suicide. Had one of the Robison family taken the lives of his/her siblings, mother and father or a parent killed their spouse and children? The theory was quickly put to rest; the evidence simply did not support the theory.

The investigators found bloody footprints in the cottage. They were made by a size 10½ shoe wearing a Tote shoe cover, leading authorities to believe there was possibly a lone killer.

Some evidence in the case had been compromised by poor police procedures. The police permitted almost anyone to enter the cottage during their investigation and a deputy even picked up and handled the hammer used to bludgeon Susan's head, thus eliminating the possibility of finding fingerprints.

Clues Lacking
6 Family Members Killed

Another problem which hampered the investigation was the 27-day period between the time the crime was committed and when the bodies were discovered. The bodies were severely decomposed by the fly larvae feeding on the bodies and excessive heat inside the cottage, any evidence outside the cottage, footprints, blood, and fingerprints had been obliterated by rain, wind and sun. And most importantly, the killer or killers had 27 days to escape and fabricate an alibi.

Several people, friends and neighbors of the Robison's, were interviewed but were unable to offer much assistance. All they knew was Mr. Robison had talked of the family's plans to fly to Kentucky on business then continue on to Florida to purchase a condominium. So when the Robison's were not seen for several weeks no one suspected anything was amiss.

Nobody questioned why the family cars were parked outside the cottage, and nobody wondered why the family wasn't seen. It was assumed the family had flown out as planned and no one suspected their dead bodies were decaying in the heat of the closed cottage under the hot July sun.

Many tips poured into the Emmet County Sheriff's Department and the Michigan State Police. Each credible tip was followed up on.

The deputies and police checked into the personal lives of the Robison family, looking for someone who might have a motive for the crime.

They found that Mr. Robison nor any of his family had ever had any altercations with the law. In fact they seemed to be the ideal family, the kids were studious and clean cut. The marriage seemed to be strong, and Mr. Robison's advertising company, RC and Associates, seemed to be a thriving, profitable concern.

There were many questions that needed answers; was the killing of the family just a senseless random act by a homicidal maniac who happened upon the Robison home? Was it a ritualistic killing by some yet unknown cult stalking northwestern Michigan?

Could the same murderer who stalked young women on the campuses of the University of Michigan and Eastern Michigan University somehow be connected with these murders? The eldest Robison son was a student at Eastern Michigan University; possibly he was a witness to a murder or an accomplice to the "Co-ed Killer" as the newspapers dubbed the murderer haunting the two campuses.

The investigation revealed that Mr. Robison was not quite the man he portrayed. They found that Mr. Robison was known to have had affairs with several women outside of his marriage.

One of his secretaries became pregnant and it was rumored to be his child. The pregnancy resulted in a miscarriage but the woman's boyfriend at the time was reported to have mob connections. Had a jealous boyfriend killed Richard and his family?

Another theory that surfaced was that a family of a client of Robison's agency also had mob connections and they were upset with how they were billed for work done by Robison's agency.

An interesting coincidence was that both scenario's involved Detroit mobsters and the weapon of choice of the mob in the late sixties was the AK-47 rifle; the same weapon the State Police Crime Lab determined was used to kill the Robison Family.

The mob connection, while interesting and intriguing, remains a possibility but not one with a high degree of probability.

Crime is not un-known in the small community of Good Hart or Emmett County, however the horrific murder of six people in their cottage along the Lake Michigan shore was unheard of. Locals would meet at the Good Hart General Store to discuss the murders. Theories were discussed, agreed to and debunked.

Some of the locals subscribed to the theory that it was Monnie Bliss, the caretaker of Summerset, who had murdered the Robison family. The authorities also took notice of Monnie.

Monnie's son, Norman, had just been killed in a motorcycle accident. The family was grieving for their son when Mr. Robison stopped by the Bliss house and asked the dead boy's mother to purchase flowers for her own son's funeral from the Robison family.

Had this insensitive, cold gesture by the wealthy landowner to his caretaker's wife been too much for Monnie and triggered a horrible vengeful killing spree?

Most agree that Monnie Bliss was a bit strange; he was sometimes found walking through the woods talking to himself or talking to his recently deceased son and Monnie even sometimes in a drunken state claimed that he indeed had killed the family. He remains a suspect, but there was one person most investigators believe was responsible for brutally massacring the family of six.

As the investigation progressed, it was discovered that Mr. Robison's business affairs might not have been as successful as initially thought. It was found that the advertising agency was guilty of some business practices that were not always above board.

Bullet-Riddled Bodies Of 6 in Family Found

The RC and Associates agency was found to be over billing clients for advertising space purchased in print media, its largest client, Delta Faucets, was a victim of this practice.

The arts magazine, "Impresario" was not all it was originally thought to be either. Robison and his partner, Joseph Scolaro, placed full page ads in the magazine for major airlines and other upscale companies without the companies knowledge or permission. They did this to give the publication the appearance of being more successful and lucrative. They also inflated the amount of issues printed to give advertisers the impression it was more prominent than it actually was.

Richard Robison was working on another business venture. He and some unknown partners were proposing to build highly automated warehouses near airports in several American cities. The people Mr. Robison was working on the project with were never identified and remain another perplexing mystery of the case.

For the months prior to the murder, the new venture had consumed Robison's attention, taking him out of town on several occasions and the day-to-day operation of the advertising agency was handed over to his partner, Joseph Scolaro.

On the day of the murder, the police estimate to be June 25, 1968, the Robison family was preparing for their flight to Kentucky where Mr. Robison was reported to be going to invest in a horse ranch. He telephoned his bank to inquire if a $200,000.00 deposit had been made in the ad agency's account.

He was told that the deposit had not been made and in fact the business account was alarmingly short of funds.

Mr. Robison knew he had not withdrawn the funds from the account and the only other person who had the authority to remove money was his partner.

There were several telephone calls made between the cottage in Good Hart and the ad agency's Southfield office on the morning of the murder. The receptionist at the agency told police that when Mr. Robison called he sounded very angry.

She also told the police that Joseph Scolaro left the agency at 10:30 AM that morning of the telephone calls and did not return that day.

Police in the Detroit area interviewed Mr. Scolaro's wife and learned that he had not returned to his home until 10:00 PM that night.

Where had Richard Robison's partner, Joseph Scolaro, been for almost eleven hours on the day of the multiple homicides?

Mr. Scolaro told the State Police he left the agency after the telephone calls with Richard and went to the plumber's convention being held at Detroit's Conference center, Cobo Hall.

The agency's primary client was Delta Faucets, the manufacturer of quality bathroom and kitchen faucets so a visit to the convention was not out of line.

Scolaro said he then went to the Hotel Pontchartrain in the downtown Detroit area and had a drink at the Salamander Bar. After the cocktail Scolaro told the investigators he went shopping and finally went home.

Joseph Scolaro, partner of Richard Robison, accounted for his time on the day the Robison family was so grizzly murdered.

But the authorities could not find any witnesses who could place Scolaro at the plumber's convention, the Salamander Bar or in the stores he said he shopped in.

Michigan State police forensic technicians determined the rifle used to kill the Robison family, Shirley, Richard, Richard Jr., Gary, Randy and daughter Susan, was a AK-47.

They also established that the handgun used to fire a shot into five of the victim's heads, as they lay on the floor of the cottage, possibly some still alive, was a Berretta pistol.

There were fifteen empty shell casings found in and around Summerset cottage; eleven from a rifle and four from a Berretta.

It was well known that Joe Scolaro was a gun aficionado; he owned several rifles, shotguns and pistols, including two AK-47s and a Berretta pistol.

Scolaro told police that one of his AK-47s was in Chicago at a friend's house; Chicago Police confiscated the weapon. Although, Scolaro could not produce the second AK-47. He said he had loaned it to his brother-in-law. However, it was never located.

Police went to a gun range that Scolaro frequented. They dug through the dirt finding shell casings from an AK-47 rifle, some of which were said to have a striking resemblance, if not matching, the casings found at the crime scene.

The investigation also revealed that Scolaro had purchased matching Berretta handguns, one for himself and he gave the other to his partner, Richard Robison.

Friends of the Robison family told the police that Richard usually took the expensive handgun to their cottage in Good Hart, Michigan.

The Emmett County Sheriff's Department searched Summerset but did not find the Berretta, they theorized that was the weapon used in the massacre of the family and then the murderer(s) took it with them.

Joseph Scolaro, Richard Robison's trusted partner, was the prime suspect in the murder of the family. He had motive since his embezzlement of company funds had been discovered. He had a means: Scolaro owned both types of weapons used in the slaughter. And Scolaro had opportunity; Scolaro was missing for eleven hours without a witness to substantiate his alibi.

Adding to the evidence mounting against him was the fact that Scolaro was given a polygraph test which indicated he was not being truthful. Also, Scolaro wore a size 10½ shoe and owned a pair of Tote shoe covers.

The Emmett County District Attorney did not issue an arrest warrant for Joseph Scolaro because he didn't feel the circumstantial evidence against the man was strong enough and it was not believed Scolaro had time to commit the crime.

More Work Needed In Murder Case

PETOSKEY (UPI) -- Emmet County Prosecutor Donald C. Noggle has indicated more work may be needed before he can request a murder warrant in the 1968 slayings of six members of the Richard C. Robison family at their plush Lake Michigan summer home near here.

The D.A. said eleven hours was simply not enough time for Scolaro to drive from the Detroit area, shoot the family, beat Susan with a claw hammer and rape Mrs. Robison's dead or dying body and return to his home by 10:00 PM that same day.

In early 1970 the bloody slaughter of the Robison family took another turn.

A prisoner serving time in Leavenworth Penitentiary in Kansas claimed to have information about the family that was murdered in northern Michigan.

Alexander Bloxom, serving time on a robbery conviction, said he was in a halfway house with a man named Mark Brock.

Bloxom says he drove Brock to a restaurant in Flint where they met with a man named "Scollata."

The convict told the police that Brock then obtained some guns and went up north with another man, Robert Mathews, in a borrowed blue car.

Bloxom said he did not go with the men because there were not many black men in the area and he would have attracted too much attention.

The men who went north brought back a briefcase filled with papers of Richard Robison and a suitcase that belonged to the family.

Mathews told the police that on the day of the murders he was out of state on gun buying trip.

Following up on the information provided by the inmate, the authorities gave Bloxom and Mathews a lie detector test.

Mathews passed his polygraph test and was able to provide witnesses to verify his presence at the out of state gun show.

The test that Bloxom agreed to indicated that he was not being truthful in his statements, destroying the little credibility that he might have had.

Mark Brock, the man Alexander Bloxom claimed to have murdered the family refuted the claims and refused to take a polygraph test.

The tip went nowhere.

On March 8, 1973, almost five years after the grizzly murder of the six members of the Robison family, the investigation again took another turn.

Two men entered the office of the advertising agency that Joseph Scolaro then owned, found the owner slumped in the chair behind his desk, the wall behind him were streaked with red blood, splinters of skull and smatterings of brain tissue.

Joseph Scolaro had used a gun from his beloved collection to shoot himself in the head.

A suicide note on his desk was addressed to his family read in part:

"Mother – where do I start…" "I am a liar – cheat – phony. Any check that any people have with your signature isn't any good, because I forged your name to get them off my back…" "I know I am sick, but getting help isn't going to help the people I've hurt."

At the end of the note was written; *"I had nothing to do with the Robisons. I am a cheat but not a murderer."*

Thirty-eight year old Joseph Scolaro left a wife and two young sons.

Close to a year from the date Scolaro took his life and his secrets to the grave, an interesting piece of evidence surfaced which seemed to support the story of the Leavenworth prisoner, Alexander Bloxom.

A Michigan State Trooper came across a 1965 blue Chevrolet with Ohio license plates seemingly abandoned on the side of M-14. In the course of searching the car a tan colored leather luggage tag was found in the glove box... The name and address on the luggage tag read:

Shirley Robison
18790 Dolores
Lathrup Village, Michigan

The owner of the car was found through registration records to be a man living in Omer, Michigan. He told authorities he had bought the car for his son to use while he was working at Cedar Point Amusement Park, in Sandusky, Ohio. He did not know anything about a luggage tag being in the glove box.

The man's son was interviewed and he informed the police that the car, a 1965 blue Chevrolet, two door was stolen from a parking lot at Cedar Point in August of 1973. He also did not know anything about a luggage tag being in the glove box.

The son said he was working with another man from the Detroit area who was fired the same day the car disappeared.

The man fired was found at his parent's home in Dearborn, Michigan. He did admit to stealing the car and when it stalled out he abandoned it on the side of M-14. He claimed to know nothing about a luggage tag in the glove box.

Had the luggage tag been planted in the car to send police in another direction? Was the luggage tag actually from Shirley Robison? Was the car used in the murder as the Leavenworth prisoner said? The owners of the car and the person who stole it were not considered to be suspects in the murder of the family. The clue of the luggage tag remains another mysterious anomaly of the Robison family murder.

As with all cold case investigations, advances in forensic technology are developing and being employed on old unsolved cases.

In 2003, thirty-five years after the murder of the Robison family, a DNA test was performed on pubic hairs found on the body of Mrs. Robison.

Authorities waited in anticipation to receive definitive evidence indicating the murderer of the six Robison's. Unfortunately, in the more than three decades since the family was found slaughtered, the pubic hairs had been damaged and conclusive identification could not be made.

The tranquil peacefulness of Good Hart, Michigan was shattered when a person shot through the window of Summerset cottage, striking Richard in the chest, stormed in and turned the assault rifle on Randy and Shirley Robison, shot Susan and the two older boys as they ran from the carnage. The cold blooded killer then shot five of the family in the head, execution style with a Berretta and took a claw hammer to 8 year old Susan making sure they were dead.

On the anniversary of the murders, the case is brought back to the forefront, local newspapers write articles rehashing the facts of the case. In the years since the senseless slaughter, a few books have been authored about the Robison murders and make a good presentation of the evidence to date, but in the almost 45 years since the murder of the family, no one has ever been brought before a judge to account for the death of Richard, Shirley, Richard Jr., Gary, Randy and Susan Robison.

The case remains open. Anyone who can be of assistance in the case should contact the Emmett County Sheriff's Department.

I Want To Be A Priest

Father Albert Kunz was the beloved pastor of St. Michael's Parish in the village of Dane, just north of Madison, Wisconsin. He was a Wisconsin boy who was born in 1931 in the town of Dodgeville, Wisconsin, one of three sons of a family who emigrated from Switzerland.

Albert knew he wanted to be a priest since the age of ten. That is when he almost died from a ruptured appendix. As he recovered, he announced to his mother, "I want to be a priest."

Albert was persistent with his passion and enrolled in the Pontifical College in Worthington, Ohio and was ceremoniously ordained into the Priesthood in 1956.

Father Kunz served as pastor for Waunakee, Cassville and Monroe, Wisconsin congregations before he arrived at St. Michael's in 1967. There he found a home and would remain at the Dane Catholic Church for thirty-one years.

The Father was a traditional priest who performed mass in both English and Latin. He was also a student of Catholicism, becoming an expert in Canon Law and serving the Diocese of Madison as the Judicial Vicar and as a member of the Catholic Marriage Tribunal where he stressed the sanctity and permanence of marriage.

Father Al, as he was affectionately called, also

Dane priest slain

was called to investigate complaints of sexual abuse of minors by priests in the Catholic Diocese of Springfield, Illinois.

In addition to all of these duties, the Good Father hosted a religious radio talk show titled, "Our Catholic Family."

At 7:00 AM on March 4, 1998, a teacher who worked at the church school arrived at the school and found Father Al in the hallway near the door to his quarters, lying in a pool of blood. He had been stabbed and his throat had been slashed, cutting the carotid artery. Father Albert Kunz had bled to death in a matter of minutes.

The sheriff's department was called to the church and began a homicide investigation that became one of the most expensive, most intense and the most far reaching than any other in the history of Dane County.

As Dane County Sheriff's Lt. Kevin Hughes said, "Trying to establish *why* Father Al was killed it would first be necessary to determine *who* had killed him."

There was no shortage of motives that the authorities were following; was his death the result of a burglary? Was Father Al murdered because of his staunch beliefs on abortion? Was it someone in the church trying to cover up a crime the Father had uncovered? Was it a ritual killing? Was it a crime that could be traced back to the hierarchy of the Catholic Church itself?

A search found all of the doors to the church and school were locked and there was no sign of forced entry. Nothing was missing; nothing seemed to be out of place. Burglary was ruled out.

Some felt that a disgruntled teacher or other employee at the school or church may have had an argument with the priest and in a fit of rage killed Father Al. At one time the police thought they may have identified a possible suspect but nothing that resulted in an arrest.

The authorities, in the course of their investigation, found that in the 1990s Father Kunz held a burial of an aborted fetus during a protest of abortion.

Had this very public protest caught the attention of extremist groups and possibly led to his death? Perhaps one of the very active pro-choice groups from nearby Madison, Wisconsin and the University of Wisconsin had taken revenge on the man who was responsible for such a public protest.

WISCONSIN STATE JOURNAL

FRIDAY/MARCH 6, 1998   MADISON, WISCONSIN   10 CENTS

Fear and rumors in wake of murder

Kunz

Investigators   By Brenda Ingersoll   adjoining St. Michael Catholic Church, Milwaukee-area church break-ins and

One of the more bizarre leads the sheriff's deputies followed up was a report that fifteen miles from St. Michael's Church just days before the priest was killed, a calf was found in its pen with its throat slit. Was there a cult in the area that had killed Father Al in some ritualistic murder?

Another path the authorities explored was Father Kunz's investigation of complaints of sexual abuse by others in the Catholic Church. It was reported that Father Kunz was going to release his findings on March 7th. The priest was murdered just three days prior, although the inquiry did not lead to the arrest of anyone or even identify anyone the police could consider a suspect.

Another intriguing course the police investigated was that Father Alfred Kunz was a friend of Malachi Martin who was an author and was known to perform exorcisms. It was also said that Father Kunz had participated in exorcisms at St. Michael's.

After the priest's death, Martin declared that Father Kunz had been killed by a group of "Luciferians."

Luciferians are those who worship Lucifer as Christians worship God. But the investigation into any Luciferians who might have murdered the priest did not turn up any solid leads.

Despite the authorities best efforts, the identity of the person or persons who viciously slit the throat of Father Al have not been found since it happened nearly 15 years ago. The case is still an active investigation for the Dane County Sheriff's Department.

Anyone with information that could assist the Sheriff's Department in solving this vicious and heinous crime are asked to contact the department immediately.

Who Killed The Boy In The Box?

Fred Benonis was driving along Susquehanna Road in Northeast Philadelphia when he saw a rabbit jump into the underbrush. He pulled to the side, stopped and chased after the animal. While looking around he came across a pile of trash. The area was known to be a dump for residents. There he noticed a large cardboard carton.

The carton, measuring 15 inches by 19 inches and 35 inches tall, had markings indicating it originally contained a baby bassinet sold through a J. C. Penney store.

Twenty-six year old Fred Benonis, a student in his junior year at LaSalle College, looked in the box and saw what he thought was a doll but then soon realized it was the body of a young child.

He left the area and ran for his car.

Fearing he would get in trouble for being in that area, he decided not to tell anyone of his discovery. Fred would later admit he sometimes stopped along the road to peek at the girls staying at the nearby Good Shepherd School for Wayward Girls.

By the next morning Fred was having feelings of guilt for concealing the discovery of a dead child. He talked with two priests who taught at the college and confided in them the gruesome find he had made. At their urging, Fred contacted the Philadelphia Police.

On February 26, 1957 the police went to the location and found the nude body of a male child in the J. C. Penney box.

The blue-eyed boy, estimated to be between four and six years old, was lying in the box, face up, arms posed across his

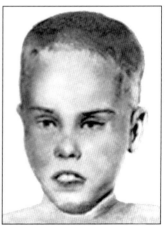

An artist rendition of the boy found dead in the box.

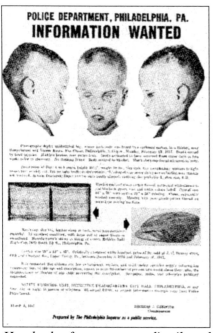

POLICE DEPARTMENT, PHILADELPHIA. PA.
INFORMATION WANTED

Hundreds of posters were distributed around the Philadelphia area seeking help in identifying the boy.

stomach, and wrapped in a flannel blanket. Oddly, the blanket had been cut in half.

Someone took measures to clean the boy, cut his blondish hair, trimmed his finger and toenails, and washed him. The youth was just over forty inches tall yet only weighed thirty pounds and appeared malnourished.

The child had several bruises all over his body, but most were on his face and head, indicating the boy's death was a homicide. There was also loose hair on his body indicating his hair was cut while the child was nude, either before or after his death.

His feet and hands were discolored and wrinkled as if they had lain in water for an extended period of time.

The police searched the area where the body was discovered and found some potential evidence; a blue corduroy man's cap that was made in Philadelphia, a men's white handkerchief embroidered with a capital "G", a tan colored child's scarf and yellow flannel shirt the size appropriate for the dead boy. Also found was a pair of shoes, size one. The shoes were tried on the boy but were too large for him to have comfortably worn.

A search of missing child files in the Philadelphia area did not reveal any children answering the description of the Boy in the Box. The police theorized the child was from another location and dumped in the northeast Philadelphia area.

The Philadelphia press dubbed the murdered child; "The Boy in the Box."

The police looked into the possibility that the boy found was Steven Damman, a youth that was kidnapped in front of a Long Island, New York supermarket in 1955.

Both boys had blue eyes and a scar under their chin and the age of the boy found in the box looked to be about the same as the kidnapped boy.

SAME CHIN SCAR

Slain Child May Be Kidnaped N.Y. Boy

The Long Island boy had a birthmark on his right calf but the leg of the Boy in the Box was too bruised to see if the birthmark existed. The footprints of the Boy in the Box were sent to Long Island authorities for comparison to footprints taken at birth of the missing New York boy.

The footprints proved to be the evidence needed to dismiss the idea that the boy found dead in the J.C. Penney box was the Long Island, New York child.

In 2003, the disappearance of Steven Damman was still unsolved and the Long Island police contacted the Philadelphia police to see if all pieces of evidence had been considered in 1957. DNA from the boy in Philadelphia was taken and compared with that of Damman family members. The test proved to be inconclusive.

Another person came forward in March of 1957 claiming he might be able to identify the child. PFC George Broomall, a Marine who recently returned from overseas was concerned the dead boy was his younger brother.

The Marine was one of 18 children from a Philadelphia family. While he was stationed overseas, his family moved to California and he was concerned something had happened to a younger brother before the family left.

The police arranged for the PFC to view the body of the Boy in the Box in the morgue to possibly identify the body.

The Marine could not make a positive identification nor could rule out that it was his brother.

After days of not knowing, word came from California police that the brother of George Broomall was with the family in California.

It was another lead that went nowhere.

In 1961, a couple was arrested for the deaths of six of their ten children. Ken and Irene Dudley, carnival workers who traveled extensively, were responsible for allowing their children to become malnourished and die. They disposed of their dead children in locations similar to where the boy was found in Philadelphia, but primarily in southern states.

The mystery boy found in the box proved not to be one of the poor children of the disgusting couple.

Not far from the dump site where the boy was found in the cardboard box that originally held a bassinet from the J.C. Penney store, was a large brick house where the couple who owned it took in foster children from state and city agencies.

The police checked out the foster home and found all children were accounted for, thus eliminating the possibility that the child found dead in the box came from the foster home.

Dead Boy May Be Marine's Brother

PHILADELPHIA (UP) — Police today checked a report by a Marine stationed at the Philadelphia Naval Base who said he was "reasonably sure" the unidentified boy found murdered in a lot last Tuesday was his brother.

In 1960, an investigator from the medical examiner's office, Remington Bistow, was investigating the cold case of the boy in the box on his own. He even enlisted the assistance of a psychic from New Jersey.

After holding a staple from the J.C. Penney box, the psychic told Mr. Bistow to look for a large house with a log cabin in the rear where children played.

The medical examiner's investigator drove miles searching for a house that might be the one the psychic described. He came across the home used as a foster home and became interested in it. The home met the details given by the psychic. It even had a pond in the back by the old log home where the child's foot and hand may have laid in the water becoming prunish.

When the home came up for sale, the auction company hosted an open house providing Bistow an opportunity to tour the house. He discovered in the basement a baby bassinet like the one that had been shipped in the J.C. Penney carton.

Outside of the home, Bistow noticed blankets hanging on the clothesline prior to the auction. The plaid blankets had been cut in half to fit the small cots on which the foster children slept. The flannel blanket covering the boy had also been cut in half.

Remington Bistow was convinced the boy found dead in the bassinet box had come from the foster home. At Bistows urging, in 1986, detectives from the Philadelphia Police Department again looked into a possible connection between the boy found murdered and the foster home. The police found nothing substantial to merit more time and manpower on a connection between the child and the foster home.

Bistow unofficially kept at the case for years to follow.

In 1998, the case was reopened and the chief of police requested that detectives look into the foster home one more time. They interviewed the owners of the foster home and again determined no evidence existed to implicate them in the death of the child.

In the fifty-five years since the un-identified boy was found lying in a cardboard carton in the weeds off Susquehanna Road in Northeast Philadelphia, many leads developed but none lead to an arrest of a person or persons who maliciously beat the malnourished boy until he died.

Someone might still be alive who has information for the police that can help them solve this cold case. It is requested that anyone that can help please call the Philadelphia Police Department.

A Brutal Beating In A Rural Setting

All too often when someone from another state thinks of Michigan, the first thought that comes to mind is the automobile factories of the Greater Detroit metropolitan area, yet Michigan is so much more.

The state offers the longest freshwater coastline of any other state, dominion, province, principality, or country in the world. Michigan is bordered by four of the Great Lakes; Lakes Michigan, Huron, Superior, and Erie. There are 64,980 inland lakes and ponds within the state; a person in the state is never more than six miles from a lake or river. The state is covered with vast forests of hard and softwoods, and the hunting and fishing is a sportsman's dream.

Winterfield Township is located in Clare County in the northern section of the state's lower peninsula where the forests are thick and the population is thin. Sidney Hildebrant, a man of seventy six years, lived by himself in a trailer on a remote section of the township.

On September 5, 1997 Hildebrant's son, Phillip, went to his visit his father and found him dead.

An autopsy revealed Sidney Hildebrant had been beaten with a blunt object, beaten so severely his jaw was broken in four places.

The investigative duties in the murder case of Sidney Hildebrant were shared by the Clare County Sheriff's Department and the Michigan State Police. Despite there being no physical evidence, the law enforcement authorities developed some suspects.

However, the suspects were forgotten in 1999 when a convicted felon, Travis Troost, told the police that he was a witness to the murder.

He and three other men, Daren Olson, Jason Conrad and Ron Balcer had gone to Hildebrant's trailer with the intention to rob him. It was rumored that Hildebrant carried large sums of money.

The three men were arrested and charged with murder and armed robbery.

At the trial in 2000 Troost testified that the three men, all in their twenties at the time, demanded money from Hildebrant. When the older man refused, the three beat him to death with some object.

Supporting the robbery theory, the police testified to the court that an empty men's wallet was found in the woods near the trailer.

On May 12, 2000 the three men were found not guilty of the murder.

The fact that the prosecutor's chief witness, Travis Troost, at the time of the trial was serving a prison sentence for home invasion and robbery did not lend credence to his testimony. Troost was reported to be a liar and his testimony did not mesh with the forensic evidence.

After the trial, it was widely thought that Troost fabricated his story in hope of being rewarded with a reduced prison sentence.

The police lost valuable time in solving the case when Troost led them on a wild goose chase. To this day the real killer / killers of 76 year-old Sidney Hildebrant have not been identified.

Anyone with any leads that can help the Hildebrant family find closure is asked to call the Michigan State Police ot the Clare County Sheriff's Department.

Why Didn't They Leave My Babies Alone?

-Loretta Grimes

The 1956 Elvis Presley movie "Love Me Tender" is a touching story of the four Reno brothers. The three oldest brothers left the family farm to fight for the Confederate Army in the Civil War and youngest brother, Clint, played by Elvis Presley, stayed home with their mother to tend the farm.

The family received false notice that the oldest brother had been killed and Clint ends up marrying the oldest brother's girlfriend. The movie traces the conflict Clint's marriage causes within the family.

It was the first movie for Elvis and teenage girls flocked to the theaters to see the gyrating heartthrob that was taking America by storm.

Barbara, age 15 and her sister Patricia, just days short of becoming a teenager, were no different than other girls their age, they could hardly wait for the movie to appear at the Brighton Theater so they could see Elvis on the big screen.

On December 28, 1956 the two sisters walked the short distance from their home on Damen Street to the theater on Archer Street.

The sisters were such big fans of the rock and roll star that this would be the eleventh time they would see "Love Me Tender."

The girls bought popcorn and sat with a classmate of Patricia's. They sank down into their seats and squealed like the rest of the teenagers when Elvis first appeared.

At the conclusion of the film the sisters walked out of the theater with Patricia's friend. The Grimes sisters said their goodbyes to the other girl and disappeared into the night. Literally, they were not seen alive again.

Barbara and Patricia should have been home by 11:45 but when the clock struck midnight and the girls were still not home the girl's mother became concerned.

Mrs. Grimes sent the girl's oldest sister and younger brother to the bus stop to wait on them. After several buses came and went and the Grimes sisters were not on board they went home to report to their mother.

The police were called and took a report but treated the disappearance of the two girls possibly as a runaway. They told Mrs. Grimes to give the girls time and they will return.

Hours turned to days and the sisters did not return. At one point Elvis made a plea to the girls to return home to their mother. The police began to investigate the disappearance in earnest. Tips and leads flooded into the police department. Citizens reported seeing the girls on their way home and some people reported seeing them in Milwaukee, Wisconsin and Nashville, Tennessee.

It was rumored the girls had left town with two sailors and also that they had left town in search of Elvis Presley.

A ransom note received by Mrs. Grimes brought in the Federal Bureau of Investigation. FBI agents accompanied her as she took a bus to Milwaukee and left a bag with $1,000 next to a pew in church. The possible kidnapper said Barbara would pick up the bag, take it to the kidnapper and she and Patricia would return.

No one appeared to retrieve the money. The person who wrote the ransom note turned out to be an institutionalized mentally disturbed individual.

Twenty-five days after they disappeared, on January 22, 1957 the bodies of the sisters were discovered.

A couple driving in the southwest section of Cook County, near Chicago, along the two lane German Church Road about a half of a mile east of County Line Road noticed something about five feet off the road.

Lying there were the bodies of the two Grimes sisters. The girls had been tossed near the culvert that carries Devil's Creek below the road.

Barbara laid on her left side, her sister's body laid face up partially covering Barbara's head. Both girls were nude.

The police estimated the bodies had been there for two weeks but had avoided detection because a heavy snow had fallen on January 9 and covered them. A mid-January thaw revealed the poor murdered children.

Evidence showed the girls had been severely beaten before their death, one of the girls had an 18 inch long welt across her back. Both girls had been stabbed with an instrument which left puncture wounds similar to those an ice pick would make. They also determined Barbara had been sexually assaulted.

The final cause of death for the fifteen and twelve year-old girls was shock due to exposure to low temperatures. Barbara and Patricia were alive when their killer left them to the cold Chicago December weather.

As the police investigated the disappearance and death of the sisters they theorized there was a maniac roaming the streets of Cook County killing

children. The year before on October 16, 1956 three boys left their Northwest Chicago home to go to a movie theater in the Loop.

On October 18, 1956 the boys were found dead in Robinson Woods, a forest preserve just beyond the cities northwest city limit.

The boys, John Schuessler, 13, his brother Anton Schuessler age 11, and 14 year old Robert Peterson were found completely nude in a shallow ditch about 100 feet east of the Des Plaines River.

They had been severely beaten leaving welts similar to those found on one of the Grimes sisters. The boy's bodies showed signs of being tied up during their captivity and tape had been placed over their eyes.

Robert Peterson, the oldest of the three boys, was strangled with a rope or some similar device. The Schuessler brothers had been suffocated.

The police thought they had found a vital clue in the death of the boys. Scrapings removed from beneath the boys fingernails revealed microscopic traces of stainless steel. In 1956 the use of stainless steel was rare. But, the discovery did not help the police find the killer of the boys.

The investigation looked for a connection between the murder of the boys found in Robinson Woods and that of the Grimes sisters. There were similarities but nothing produced solid leads.

The murders of John and Anton Schuessler, and Robert Peterson went unsolved for decades. In 1994, almost 40 years later, the police arrested Kenneth Hanson for the abduction, torture and murder of the three boys. In 1995 he was found guilty and sentenced to 200 – 300 years in prison.

The abduction of Barbara and Patricia in 1956 was not connected to the murder of the boys. The hundreds and possibly thousands of hours devoted to connecting the murders was all for nothing.

The person or persons who tormented and threw the two girls to the side of the road while they were still alive, leaving them to die in the subfreezing temperatures have never been found. Probably the killer is dead by now or possibly had committed other crimes and rotted in jail, but they were never found guilty of the senseless murder of two innocent fifteen and twelve year old girls.

A Parent's Worst Nightmare

....

A serial killer stalked Oakland County, Michigan, a northern suburb of Detroit. The murderer snuffed the life out of at least four children before the killings stopped as mysteriously as they began.

On February 15, 1976, twelve year-old Mark Stebbins was spending Sunday with his mother at the Ferndale American Legion hall. Mark grew bored and asked his mother if he could go home and watch television.

Mark's mother agreed and the boy started off on the nine-block walk home. He didn't arrive.

Parents, police, volunteers and friends mounted a search for young Mark but he unfortunately could not be found.

On February 19, 1976, just four days after Mark Stebbins disappeared, his fully clothed body was found in the parking lot of a Southfield, Michigan shopping center.

An office worker noticed something off the parking lot and found the body of the boy neatly laid along a brick retaining wall in a pile of weeds and snow.

The Southfield Police Department took charge of the investigation of the boy. They had the body removed from the parking lot and taken to the police department office where the clothing was removed before the boy's body was sent to the morgue. The clothing was searched for trace evidence.

The police determined Mark was killed somewhere else and his body was placed at the parking lot. His death occurred approximately the day before his body was found.

There were rope abrasions on his neck and hands indicating he was abducted and held captive prior to his death. The evidence further revealed that Mark Stebbins had been strangled and sexually assaulted with some type of object.

Almost nine months later, on December 22, 1976 twelve-year-old Jill Robinson argued with her mother and packed her backpack and ran away from her Royal Oak home.

The following day Jill's bicycle was found behind a store on Main Street in the city, but it offered little valuable evidence.

Four days later on December 26, 1976, the day after Christmas, the bloody body of Jill Robinson was found along interstate I-75 near Big Beaver Road in Troy, Michigan. The neatly laid out body could be seen from the Troy Police Department.

Jill, only 12 years-old, had been shot in the face with a shotgun and laid out neatly and fully clothed. She even still wore her backpack. Dental records were necessary to make a positive identification.

The abduction and murder of the two children in the suburban Detroit area made parents more conscientious of where their children went, how they traveled and with whom they went.

Schools tightened security and made calls to parents to check on students who were absent without parents first contacting the school.

Parents drove their children to and from school, and drove or accompanied their children any place they went. Both parents and schools instructed children in the importance of not talking to strangers and to turn and run if someone should try to entice them into a car.

Just days after the discovery of the body of Jill Robinson, another child disappeared. On January 2, 1977 a ten year-old girl, Kristine Mihelich, was abducted in Berkley, Michigan another Oakland County city.

Kristine was last seen at a 7-Eleven on Twelve Mile Road buying a magazine. She was missing for two and a half weeks before her body was found discarded in the snow on the side of a rural road in Oakland County's Franklin Village.

She had been neatly laid out within view of homes on the road. She was fully dressed, her eyes were closed and her arms were folded across her chest. Ten year-old Kristine had been smothered to death.

The next child victim was eleven year-old Timothy King. On March 16, 1977 about 8:30 PM Tim walked, his skateboard under his arm, to a drugstore on Maple Road in his city of Oakland County's Birmingham. He bought some candy with the money he had borrowed from his sister, walked out the back door of the store to a parking lot and was never seen alive again.

Timmy's abduction, coupled with the disappearance and murder of the other children, prompted a search that included Oakland County and adjoining Wayne County. Newspaper headlines shouted for the return of the boy, Timmy's father made a passionate appeal to the kidnapper to return his son unharmed, and in an open letter printed in the *Detroit News*, Mrs. King pleaded with the maniac who took her son to let him go so she could treat him to his favorite meal, Kentucky Fried Chicken.

Six days after he disappeared, two teenagers driving along Gill Road in Wayne County's city of Livonia, noticed what appeared to be a body. It was Timmy.

Laying about 300 feet from busy Eight Mile Road, the border between Oakland and Wayne Counties, laid the posed body of Timmy King, his skateboard lying next to him, clothes washed and neatly pressed.

Marks on his hands and feet showed he had been bound while being held captive.

An autopsy determined Timmy had been smothered to death only hours before he was found and he was sexually molested with an unknown object. The autopsy also revealed that Timmy's last meal was his favorite, fried chicken. The boy's body had been recently bathed.

The death of Timmy was the seventh murder of a child since January of 1976. The homicide of Cynthia Cadieux a sixteen year old that went missing from Roseville, Michigan and found in Bloomfield Township on January 16, 1976 is suspected to be by the same murderer because there are some similarities but the police are inclined to say Cynthia was killed by another person.

Another youth from Oakland County that was initially thought to be the victim of the same person who killed the four children was fourteen year old Sheila Srock.

While Sheila was baby sitting at a home in Birmingham, Michigan she was raped and shot to death. Her death was ultimately determined to be caused by a man named Oliver Rhodes, a person who could not have committed the other murders.

The evidence supported the fact that four, possibly five, if more evidence leads investigators to include Cynthia Cadieux, of the child murders were committed by the same person.

Terror and mass hysteria reigned in the Detroit Metropolitan area. Parents stormed city council and school board meetings demanding the police do more to find the fiend who was murdering their children.

Parents volunteered to stand on street corners both before and after school to ensure the children arrived safely. Schools taught lessons in "Stranger Danger," a course designed to warn children of the dangers of strangers. Students from Kindergarten to high school were warned to be in groups if they needed to walk and not to get into cars with strangers.

As evidence became public, it was reported by the press that each of the four children had been bathed prior to their deaths. The newspapers dubbed the murderer as the "Babysitter Killer" for the care the murderer provided his captives before killing them.

Oakland County Sheriff, Johannes Spreen, publically lashed out at police agencies of Oakland and Wayne Counties.

The Sheriff said he believed because of inter-jurisdictional jealousies, the investigation was fragmented and resulted in missed opportunities to catch the villain or villains who were killing the children of Oakland county.

He said local agencies lacked experience in homicide and it hindered the investigation.

Sheriff Spreen pointed out inadequacies in the case of Mark Stebbins. The police department where Mark was found did not call in the Oakland County nor the Michigan State Police crime labs, rather they handled the collection of evidence themselves. They took the body to the precinct to search the boy's clothes rather than take the body to the morgue for a thorough forensic examination.

Information was not shared between the police departments. As the Sheriff said, departments worked independently, not sharing evidence and suspects in hopes of cracking the case themselves.

The law enforcement agencies involved in the murder of Mark Stebbins were the Ferndale PD from where he disappeared and the Southfield PD where he was found.

In the abduction and shotgun murder of Jill Robinson, the Royal Oak Police investigated her disappearance and the Troy Police investigated her death.

The police in Berkley, Michigan, where Kristine Mihelich lived, were involved in her death as well as the police of Franklin Village where she was found.

There were two other local police agencies working the case of the missing children. They are the Birmingham Police Department where eleven year-old Timmy King lived and the Livonia PD where his body was discovered.

In addition to these six local police agencies, the Michigan State Police and the Sheriff's departments from both Oakland and Wayne Counties were involved.

The investigation lacked a coordinated effort in finding the murderer. Too many clues were jealously kept secret.

To counter this lack of coordination, a Task Force was formed to solely investigate deaths of the four children. The task force, under the direction of State Police Lt. Robert Robertson, was made up of Troopers from the

Michigan State Police, representatives from local police agencies and county departments. The Task Force received more that 7,000 tips through their hotline.

Evidence of the case of the four deaths lead investigators to some theories. The person or persons responsible for the deaths of the children over a 13 month period was attracted to youngsters 10 to 12 years of age. The murderer also sexually assaulted the male victims but not the females and he/they left the bodies cleaned and posed in funeral positions.

Another fact was that the murderer had the ability to hide the victims for up to 19 days before killing them. The killer might be influenced by snow, for each of the four children were found dead on days that it snowed.

The Police developed a profile of the person who was killing the children. They determined the person might be a white male between the ages of 20 to 35 years, probably intelligent and well educated, works in a white collar position that allows him freedom of movement and lives or works in Oakland county. The authorities also thought the murderer may appear to the children as someone they need not fear, such as a clergyman, a police officer or a doctor.

Dr. Bruce Danto, a psychiatrist who consulted with the Task Force was mailed a letter from a man named Allen. Allen said his roommate was suffering from post dramatic stress syndrome from having to kill children during the Vietnam War. It was his roommate who was the killer of the

Oakland county children. Allen also said he had helped his roommate by looking after the children.

A short time later Allen called the psychiatrist asking for immunity for any crimes he may have committed in exchange for providing photographic evidence of his roommates murderous ways.

The doctor and Allen agreed to meet at a Palmer Woods bar but Allen never showed up nor did he ever contact the doctor again.

The police Task Force investigating the serial murders of four Oakland county children developed a short list of suspects. Among them were Ted Lamborgine and Chris Busch, although neither was ever arrested or prosecuted for the crimes.

Lamborgine lived in the northern Detroit suburban of Royal Oak in the late 1970s and was arrested in 2007 in Ohio. He pleaded guilty to 15 counts of sex related crimes rather than take the prosecutor's offer of a lighter sentence if he would take a polygraph test related to the Oakland county child murders.

The other suspect that gained the interest of the authorities was Chris Busch, a person who had been in police custody for involvement in a child pornography ring. Although the police could not find evidence to arrest Busch, he remained a prime suspect.

Chris Busch died in 1978.

After receiving more than 18,000 tips, about two dozen arrests on unrelated charges and breaking up a multi-state child pornography ring, the Task Force disbanded in December 1978 and the investigation became the jurisdiction of the Michigan State Police.

In October 2010, some 34 years after Mark Stebbins was abducted and found murdered, the police talked via telephone with a man who only identified himself as "Bob."

Bob said he had been researching the murders of the children and wanted to share his conclusions with the authorities. He said he had several leads he wanted to share. The first was that he believed the murders might have been committed by a cult, or a group of adults and the deaths were timed to correspond with pagan holidays or in conjunction with the lunar calendar.

Bob also said he thought the murderers were abducting and dumping the bodies in specific cities. Possibly using first initial of each city to spell out a word or acronym. However, Bob said he did not know what the word or acronym was.

Bob, who said he was not involved with the killings but had a person he suspected, although, he also refused to reveal the suspect's name or to meet with the police. He said he would help the police with the investigation if they provided him information.

Bob wanted to know if Allen, the man who claimed his roommate had held the kids captive had hand written the letters he sent to Dr. Bruce Danto or typed them and from where they were mailed.

The police said they would not provide any information because they were conducting an ongoing investigation and did not want to jeopardize it in any way.

In 2012, the Babysitter Murders again were in the headlines and featured on radio and television stations. Attorney, Paul Hughs filed a $100 million law suit against The Chief Assistant Oakland County Prosecutor, Paul Walton, The Oakland County Undersheriff Mike McCabe, The Oakland County Sheriff, Michael Buchard, and the Michigan State Police. The suit was on behalf of Debora Jarvis, the mother of Kristine Mihelich, one of the children that was killed.

At the time of this writing no further information about Bob nor the lawsuit is available.

To this day the person responsible for the senseless murder of the Babysitter Killings has yet to be arrested, tried and incarcerated. Anyone with any evidence, no matter how insignificant, are asked to contact the nearest Michigan State Police post or any local or county law enforcement agency.

I Think They Have Killed Marilyn

The fourth of July is the celebration of the signing of the Declaration of Independence in 1776. It's the birthday of the United States of America, a day of picnics, parades, fireworks, and of gathering with family and friends.

On July 3, 1954, there was a small gathering of friends at 21924 Lake Road in the affluent western Cleveland suburb of Bay Village, Ohio, a sort of Fourth of July pre-party.

The home was built on a bluff offering beautiful vistas of Lake Erie from the screen-enclosed porch. But the Fourth of July celebration planned for the Lake Road house would turn into a gathering of police and the county coroner.

On that afternoon in 1954, the owners of the house, a physician and his wife, Sam and Marilyn Sheppard hosted a dinner for friends, Don and Nancy Ahern and their two children.

The two couples had cocktails and dined on the screened in porch overlooking the lake. Afterward the Ahern children were taken home and the Sheppard's son taken to bed, then the four adults settled down to watch a movie on television.

Thirty-year-old Sam sat on the couch with Marilyn cuddling close, but he had worked all day in the emergency room and was exhausted. He excused himself and laid down on a daybed off the living room and fell fast asleep before the movie was over.

Shortly after midnight the Aherns left and Marilyn spoke briefly to her husband but left him to sleep in the living room and went upstairs to bed.

During the night the doctor awoke to the sound of his wife screaming his name; "Sam!"

Through his half asleep mind, he ran up the stairs thinking his wife might be having a convulsion, as she had earlier in her pregnancy, she was in her fourth-month.

In the dim light of the bedroom Sam was startled to see a person dressed in light colored clothing standing at the foot of his wife's bed. He could also hear a gurgling noise coming from the direction of the bed.

As the doctor entered the room, he was struck on the back of the neck rendering him unconscious and he collapsed to the floor.

When Dr. Sheppard came to, he reached up to the bed feeling Marilyn's throat for a pulse and finding none, he ran down the hall to the room of their seven-year-old Chip. His son was asleep and unharmed.

Trying to clear his head while stumbling down the stairs, the doctor observed the intruder just leaving the house through the back door, running towards Lake Erie.

The person was dressed in dark clothing, leading Sheppard to believe there were possibly two intruders, one in light colored clothes that he saw upstairs another dressed in dark clothing.

Sam ran down the stairs towards the lake in pursuit of the man he felt had just killed his wife. On the beach Sam lunged for the tall, bushy-haired man, as Dr. Sheppard described the intruder, and they fell to the beach fighting.

The struggle was brief and the doctor ended up on the beach near the breaking surf, again unconscious.

Some time later, in the early morning hours, Sam regained consciousness, finding himself lying on the beach awash in the surf, his shirt and his watch missing. Dr. Sam Sheppard, in a state of confusion and pain, climbed the stairs back up to the house and ran upstairs to the bedroom.

He looked at his wife of nine years. She was lying on the bed, her breasts and her pubic area exposed. He pulled the sheet up to cover her exposed genitals.

At 5:40 AM, in a state of confusion, he could only remember the telephone number of his friend and mayor of Bay Village, Spence Houk.

"My God, Spence, get over here quick," Sam shouted into the telephone, "I think they have killed Marilyn."

Spence Houk and his wife Esther quickly drove the short distance to the Sheppard house and found Sam sitting in a chair in the den, no shirt and his pants still wet from the surf on the beach.

Minutes later a Bay Village Police officer arrived. He found a relatively incoherent husband mumbling a story of finding a man standing over his wife's bed, getting knocked out, then chasing the man to the beach where he was again rendered unconscious. They also found Marilyn Sheppard in her bed, brutally beaten to death. Marilyn Reese Sheppard was 30 years old.

Mrs. Sheppard was found lying on her back in bed, about three feet from the headboard, her head turned to the right, blood from her wounds soaked the sheet. Her pajama top had been pulled up exposing her breasts. The

Dr. Sam Sheppard

bottoms had been pulled off her left leg, the sheet Sam pulled over her covered her from the waist down.

The footboard of the bed had a horizontal wooden crossbar. Marilyn had been dragged towards the foot of the bed so that she lay with her thighs beneath the wood crossbar, feet hanging off the end of the bed, legs spread.

The walls and closet doors of the bedroom were splattered with red stains as the intruder savagely beat Marilyn's face and head. Her face was covered in blood from the more than twenty curved gashes on her face and head, leaving her almost unrecognizable.

Sam Sheppard was born in Cleveland, Ohio, the youngest of Dr. Richard Sheppard's three sons. Sam excelled in academics and athletics in Cleveland Heights High School, lettering in basketball, football and track. He was offered several athletic scholarships to Ohio colleges but chose to pursue a medical career, as did his father and two older brothers. After completing his undergraduate work he was accepted into medical school and completed his internship and residency in neurosurgery at Los Angeles County General.

While living in California, Dr. Sheppard married his high school sweetheart on February 21, 1945 in Hollywood. A few years later the couple moved back to Cleveland where Dr. Sheppard joined his father and brother's medical practice.

Marilyn Reese Sheppard. From the author's collection.

After high school graduation, Marilyn had gone off to Saratoga Springs to attend Skidmore College.

Marilyn adapted to life as the wife of a prominent and wealthy doctor. She was involved in the community and taught Bible lessons at their Methodist church.

The couple, both athletic, were active in golf and water skiing on Lake Erie. They also loved to entertain friends at their beautiful lake front home. Marilyn was four months pregnant with the couple's second child and having some health concerns. She suffered from anxiety since she had come close to dying during the birth of her first child.

The couple seemed to have the perfect life. They were wealthy, respected, healthy, vibrant young people in the prime of their lives. They had a son, Samuel Sheppard Jr., called "Chip," and another child on the way. Yet Marilyn had been bludgeoned beyond recognition, her husband left a widow and their son left motherless.

A police officer that was one of the first to arrive walked the stairs towards the lake. He went down as far as the deck at the beach house level where he could see down the beach in both directions. In his official report the officer said the sand of the beach did not look as though a struggle had occurred there, nor did he see any footprints. However, he also added that the waves were washing much of the four or five foot wide beach.

In his report, he indicated there were no signs of the intruder breaking and entering the home. He also reported that there were not any signs of a struggle in the house.

The officer also observed small puddles of water near the top of the backyard stairway, in the living room, and the stairway leading up to the bedrooms.

There were signs that the perpetrator had searched the house for valuables; the drawers of the small secretary desk in the living room were pulled open and ransacked, Sam's black leather doctor's bag was dumped on the floor, the larger desk in the study also appeared to have been rifled through.

Had the house been searched by an intruder during a robbery or was it staged, giving the appearance of a robbery?

A neighbor and friend of the Sheppards, Otto Graham, the legendary quarterback of the Cleveland Browns, stopped by the house to see what all the commotion was about. The police walked Graham through the house including into the bedroom to see Mrs. Sheppard's corpse even though it was a murder scene.

Sam Sheppard's watch and key chain were found stuffed in a green bag on a bluff above Lake Erie not far from the family's house. Dr. Sheppard could not explain why they were missing or why they found where they were.

Since the Bay Village Police Department was not accustomed to investigating murder cases, police from nearby Cleveland were called in to assist. The Cleveland coroner arrived at the Lake Road home and observed the body, took notes and asked that the body be moved to the morgue for a full autopsy.

Sam Sheppard was taken by his brother to the hospital to be treated for the beating he had received at the hands of the murderer.

A police sketch of the man with bushy hair.

Cleveland newspapers carried the news of the murder across the front page. The case involving the savage murder of the wife of the handsome, prominent Cleveland physician drew the attention of newspapers local and around the country.

While at the hospital, without his attorney present Sam was interviewed by the police. He was adamant in his innocence. But from the beginning, the police were treating the murder as a case of domestic violence. They suspected Dr. Sam Sheppard had killed his wife then fabricated the story of a lone figure, possibly two, who severely beat his wife and twice beat the young athletic doctor into unconsciousness.

The police asked Sam why Koko, the family dog, didn't bark when the intruder first entered the house and wake him up. He said that he didn't know why the dog didn't bark, he woke up only when he heard his wife call out his name.

The investigators found that the Sheppard's marriage was not on as solid ground as it appeared. The doctor had been having an affair with a nurse from the hospital, something the doctor denied but the nurse, under questioning, admitted had gone on for several years. There were other indiscretions in his past as well.

The police interviewed anyone who might have been at the home in previous weeks, including a 24-year old man, Richard Eberling who had

45

Sheppard Admits Memory Lapses

* * * *   * * * *   * * * *

Doctor Becomes Angry At Coroner's Questions

recently been at the home washing windows. The window washer related to police that the dog had not barked at him when he entered the house to wash the windows.

The investigation went on for days. The newspapers who shared the authorities opinion about Sam's guilt, wanted to know why Sam Sheppard had not been arrested. Editorials demanded the coroner to hold an inquest to determine if the evidence supported the arrest of Sheppard.

Other editorials questioned why authorities were dragging their feet, was the family of wealthy and prominent doctors exerting pressure on the authorities and slowing, if not trying to prevent, the investigation?

Whether it was due to the newspapers getting the populace riled up, or if he had done his due diligence and was ready to make a move, the day after a scathing front page editorial in the *Cleveland Press*, Coroner Gerber announced he would hold an inquest on July 22, 1954, to determine if there were grounds to arrest Dr. Sam Sheppard in the murder of his wife.

After the sensational inquest, resembling a circus more than a judicial procedure to determine the medical cause and circumstance of a death, on July 30, 1954, Dr. Sam Sheppard was arrested for the murder of his wife.

The investigation continued until August when Sheppard was indicted by a Grand Jury, his bail was reversed and the doctor was again arrested.

Cleveland and the world were intrigued by the sensational trial that began in October 1954. Press from around the country and celebrity newscasters such as Dorothy Kilgallen and Walter Winchell were in court to report to their viewers the latest on the thrilling trial.

A seven man and five woman jury was selected to hear the case against Dr. Sheppard. As expected, the defense made several motions that the presiding judge, Judge Edward Blythin, denied.

Starting on November 4, 1954 the prosecution and the defense made their opening statements, then the county prosecutor presented the case against Dr. Sam Sheppard by calling several witnesses to the stand; Officer Fred Drenkan, the first to arrive on the scene, Dr. Lester Adelson, a pathologist who stated Marilyn Sheppard died from the injuries she sustained in the beating, Coroner Dr. Sam Gerber, the man who first inspected the body and surroundings and circumstances of the murder, Mary Cowan, a Medical Technologist from the Cuyahoga County Coroner's office and twenty four year old Susan Hayes, the woman who admitted to having a several year affair with Sam Sheppard.

The defense was next to present its case before the jury. Lead attorney, Bill Corrigan, in an effort to show that the injuries Sam Sheppard sustained during the attack were actual, called four doctors and three nurses who treated

Final Arguments Today In Sheppard Case; Blythin To Charge Jurors Tomorrow

By JACK LOTTO

Sam at Bay View Hospital the day of the murder. They all indicated that the pain Sam Sheppard appeared to be in was real and they observed a possible fracture in his second cervical vertebra, swelling at the base of the skull and spasms in his neck.

On December 9, 1954 Attorney Corrigan called Sam Sheppard to the stand to testify in his own defense. His testimony had not differed much from what he had related to the police on the night of the murder.

Judge Blythin charged the jury with their deliberation responsibilities on December 17. The jury returned December 21, 1954 and declared Dr. Sam Sheppard… "Not guilty of murder in the first degree.

Then the jury announced they found Doctor Sheppard guilty of murder in the second degree.

Dr. Sam Sheppard was sentenced to life in prison!

As would be expected in such an important trial, attorney Bill Corrigan filed paperwork for an appeal.

On July 15, 1955 the Eighth District Ohio Court of Appeals affirmed the conviction.

The following year the case was taken before the Ohio Supreme Court. The Supreme Court determined there were no grounds for a new trial.

After the defense team exhausted all appeals, Sam Sheppard began life in a maximum-security prison near Columbus, Ohio.

However after a few years, new evidence came to light in the murder of Marilyn Sheppard.

During the appeal process, a noted criminal investigator determined the person who so savagely beat Marilyn Sheppard was left-handed and the weapon used was most likely a flashlight. He also discovered blood in the bedroom that, according to blood types, could not have come from either Marilyn or Sam.

In 1955, a person swimming in Lake Erie near the Sheppard house discovered a dented flashlight on the lakes bottom.

In November of 1959, Richard Eberlng, the man who was hired to wash windows at the Sheppard Lake Road house, was arrested for larceny. A ring belonging to Marilyn Sheppard was found in the Eberling house. Upon questioning, Eberling said he had robbed the Sheppard's, although, a polygraph test given to Richard Eberling to determine if he was responsible for the death of Marilyn was inconclusive.

After the death of Sam Sheppard's defense attorney, Bill Corrigan, a new defense attorney, F. Lee Bailey was hired.

F. Lee Bailey doggedly pursued what he considered a wrongful conviction. He filed petitions stating that the pretrial publicity, and the circus atmosphere of the trial violated Dr. Sheppard's right to due process.

His efforts paid off on July 15, 1964 when a judge threw out the conviction on the grounds the 1954 trial was "a mockery of justice." Sam Sheppard was released from prison.

It also came out that the judge in the first case told Dorothy Kilgallen before the trial started, "Well, he's guilty as hell. There's no question about it."

The remark was not made public by Miss Kilgallen until after the judge's death.

However, the good life for Sam Sheppard was not long lived. The State filed a petition with the Sixth Circuit Court of Appeals. On March 4, 1965 the three judges of the Court of Appeals voted to reverse the previous judges decision to throw out the conviction.

Dr. Sheppard was allowed to remain free on bail while the case was being appealed, again to the Ohio Supreme Court.

The Ohio Supreme Court, on June 6, 1966, almost 12 years after the horrendously brutal beating death of Marilyn, on a 8-1 vote reverses Dr. Sam Sheppard's murder conviction and sets him free...again.

The state was adamant in its belief that Dr. Sam Sheppard had viciously murdered his wife and mother of his son and unborn child in the early morning hours of July 4, 1954 and on October 24, 1966 began a second murder trial of the doctor.

During the trial, F. Lee Bailey pointed out that there was large blood splatter on the closet door and when tested it was found to be the same blood type as Marilyn but different from Sam's. However, the splatter also contained other properties that proved it could not have come from Marilyn, indicating there was a third person in the bedroom on the night of the murder.

Attorney Bailey brought up the fact that Richard Ebering had admitted to stealing a cocktail ring from the Sheppard house but he believed Ebering was cleared of the murder by his lie detector test. F. Lee Bailey presented a totally different possible scenario for the murder.

Defense attorney Bailey suggested that Mr. Houk the mayor of Bay Village and friend of Sam Sheppard, was having an affair with Marilyn

Sheppard. He further suggested that it was possible that Esther Houk, wife of the mayor, slaughtered Marilyn in a fit of rage over the extramarital activity.

In the second trial, Bailey did not let his client take the stand in his own defense.

On November 16, 1966, twelve years after the death of Marilyn, the jury finds Dr. Sam Sheppard ... not guilty. He is a free man... again.

Life as a free man proved to be difficult for Sam Sheppard. He practiced medicine for a while but the stress of the trials, public scrutiny, years in prison and acute alcoholism took its toll on him. Sam called on his past athleticism and attempted a career as a professional wrestler for a while.

Dr. Sam Sheppard, the person voted most likely to succeed at Cleveland Heights High School, died at the age of 46 of liver disease on April 6, 1970.

In 1989 Richard Eberling's name again came up in connection with the murder of Marilyn Sheppard. He was convicted in murdering an older widow he had befriended. The press jumped on the possible connection in the 1989 murder and the 1954 Sheppard killing.

Eberling helped fuel the fire but stopped short of ever admitting his guilt in the death of Marilyn Sheppard.

The only person brought before a jury of his own peers and convicted for the murder of Marilyn Sheppard was Marilyn's husband of nine years, Dr. Sam Sheppard. But, in a subsequent trial he was found innocent of the crime.

The popular television series, *The Fugitive*, which appeared from 1963 – 1967 and the subsequent 1993 major movie of the same name, were thought to be loosely based on the Marilyn Sheppard murder case, although the producers denied any connections between the two.

To this date no one other than her husband has been found guilty of the vicious bludgeoning death of Marilyn Sheppard.

Who Shot Michael Lovejoy?

The world of manufacturing has become streamlined to help cut costs. One strategy the automobile industry and other industries as well employ is "Just in Time Production."

In Just in Time Production, the manufacturer purchases parts from vendors and instead of having them delivered in one large shipment, has the parts delivered, as they are needed. That way the manufacturer does not need to provide warehouse space or incur other expenses that would be associated with carrying inventory.

In order for the strategy to work, Just In Time Production requires constant communication between the manufacturer, the parts vendor, and transportation companies, be it trucked or shipped by railroad.

In 1994, RTS Transport, Inc. was a trucking company that was contracted to transport truck axles from the American Axle & Manufacturing plant in Buffalo, New York to the General Motors Corporation Truck and Bus assembly plant in Pontiac, Michigan.

On April 9, 1994, one of the RTS drivers, Michael Lovejoy, was found in his truck on the side of the highway… shot to death.

Michael Lovejoy, husband and father of one child, was employed by RTS Transport, Inc. for just five weeks prior to his death.

On April 8, 1994, Lovejoy left his Flint, Michigan home driving a white 1991 GMC tractor pulling a white trailer to the American Axle & Manufacturing plant in Buffalo, New York.

His trailer was loaded and according to company records he departed the plant just before 11:00 in the morning. He guided his white RTS tractor and trailer from Buffalo, up to Niagara Falls where he crossed the Queenston – Lewis Bridge into Canada at 12:20 PM.

The shortest route from Buffalo to Michigan is through Ontario rather than driving along the southern shore of Lake Erie through New York, Pennsylvania and Ohio.

Great Lakes Cold Case Files...

The cargo of axles Michael Lovejoy was transporting was expected at 10:00 PM at the GMC Truck and Bus plant in Pontiac, Michigan, approximately thirty miles northwest of Detroit.

His route would take him across the Canadian Province via the 403, 401 and 402 highways to Sarnia, Ontario where he would cross the Bluewater Bridge into the United States at Port Huron, Michigan. From there he would follow I-69 west and then head south to Pontiac.

Around 1:30 – 1:45 PM, Michael Lovejoy pulled his white tractor-trailer onto the westbound shoulder of Highway 403 about a mile east of Wayne Gretzky Parkway near Brantford, Ontario.

Apparently Mr. Lovejoy took off his shoes and socks, set his wristwatch alarm for 5:30 and crawled into the tractor's sleeper for a nap before continuing on.

Witnesses reported seeing another white tractor-trailer parked behind Lovejoy's for a while. The truck reportedly had markings similar if not identical to those on Michael Lovejoy's RTS truck. Witnesses further said an unidentified man was seen walking from Lovejoy's tractor to the tractor-trailer parked behind his.

Thirty-five year-old Michael Lovejoy was found in the sleeper of his RTS tractor, shot several times.

The Brantford, Ontario Police Service asks persons who have any information about the person or persons who murdered Michael Lovejoy to call them or call Crimestoppers at 1-800-222-TIPS.

The Handsome Doctor And The Beautiful Widow

....

"If you seek a pleasant Peninsula, look about you."

The State of Michigan's motto aptly describes the peninsula's of the state. The Upper Peninsula is situated between Lake Superior to the north and Lakes Michigan and Huron to the south. The Upper Peninsula is sparsely populated and blessed with vast plush forests of soft and hardwoods, waterfalls and natural beauty.

The Lower Peninsula is bordered by the length of Lake Michigan on its west coast and Lake Huron and Lake St. Clair to the east.

Saginaw Bay, projecting from Lake Huron into the state's interior gives the state's Lower Peninsula its distinctive "Mitten" shape.

The "Thumb" area of the mitten, which is another peninsula, is blessed with rich soil making it some of the best agricultural land in the state. Laying between Saginaw Bay and Lake Huron the "Thumb's" climate is ideal for crops such as corn, soybeans and sugar beets. Recently the Thumb area has become Michigan's wind turbines capitol since hundreds of wind generators have been constructed to harvest the energy of the wind.

In 1908, in the "Thumb" village of Ubly, a small rural farming town, a 48-year-old farmer, John Sparling, took ill after working in the fields.

He was bent over in severe abdominal pain. His sons got him home and called Dr. Robert MacGregor.

Dr. MacGregor was the Sparling family doctor but he and his wife Ida were also good friends of John and Carrie Sparling. The couples socialized and spent much time together.

John Sparling's pain ran throughout his body and nothing the doctor did seemed to lessen it or slow it's progression. Not being able to help John, Dr. MacGregor sent him to the hospital at Port Huron, Michigan. Within days the once strong, healthy and vibrant John Sparling had died.

The cause of death was determined by the family physician to be creeping paralysis due to acute inflammation of the spine.

After John's sudden illness and death, Mrs. Sparling and her four adult sons continued to work the farm and Dr. MacGregor frequently stopped by the Sparling farm to assist with financial advice and check on the health of the Widow Sparling. The farm continued to thrive and be one of the more profitable in the area.

Dr. Robert MacGregor. From the Huron Daily Tribune, *Bad Axe, Michigan.*

One piece of financial advice Dr. MacGregor offered was that Carrie Sparling should purchase life insurance policies on her sons. Since the boys were so vital to the operation of the farm, the doctor thought they should be covered under a life insurance policy of $1,000 each just in case something should happen to them. She agreed and purchased life insurance policy's for her sons.

Two years after John Sparling was struck with a sudden strange and fatal illness, the oldest son of Carrie Sparling, Peter, came down with a painful stomach ailment with similar symptoms as his father.

Peter was working in the fields when he got pains in his stomach and became nauseous. The pains worsened and he doubled over in pain and dropped to the ground. His brothers took him home and put him in bed.

Mrs. Sparling remembered the symptoms of her husband and called the doctor.

Doctor MacGregor visited the Sparling home over the next few days, checking on Peter's condition. When he did not improve, Dr. MacGregor ordered Peter to the hospital. Despite the efforts of the doctor and the hospital staff, Peter died five days after being taken ill.

The official cause of death was sunstroke and blood poisoning.

Twenty-three year old Albert was the next member of the family to be taken ill. In May of 1911, Albert became ill with nausea, severe stomach pains, and vomiting, the same symptoms as his older brother and father displayed before their deaths.

Albert died a few days later. The doctor knew Albert had fallen a few days earlier and determined Albert's cause of death to be the result of a stomach injury he had incurred when he fell.

In a matter of three years, three members of the Sparling family had died a painful and agonizing death. People began to talk. Were the men carrying some virus that remained dormant for decades then became active and killed them? Was there something on the Sparling farm that made the men sick? People wondered if the other Sparling boys, twenty-one-year old Ray and twenty-year-old Scyril, would fall victim to the mysterious illness.

The two remaining sons of the late John and Carrie Sparling wondered too if they would be the next to die. They didn't have to wait long for the answer.

Just weeks after the death of Albert, Carrie Sparling's youngest son, Scyril began to experience stomach discomfort. Doctor MacGregor came to the Sparling house to examine the boy and he prescribed the boy a bismuth mixture to aid in his stomach discomfort. While Scyril wasn't as ill as the other Sparling men had been, he did display some symptoms similar to his father and brothers.

The following day Dr. MacGregor brought another doctor, Dr. Herrington, to consult on Scyril. Dr. Herrington examined the boy but didn't find him to be seriously ill.

The next day, Dr. MacGregor brought yet another doctor, Dr. Conboy, to the Sparling home for a consultation. The doctors found that Scyril was not improving in fact he seemed sicker than he was the day before. He had severe stomach pains, like his father and brothers.

After the examination of Scyril the doctors conferred in another room. Dr. MacGregor asked Dr. Conboy if he thought the Sparling boy could be suffering from arsenic poisoning?

MacGregor also confided to Dr. Conboy that he suspected the other Sparling men might have been poisoned as well. Although he did not say it directly, Dr. Conboy thought that Dr. MacGregor suspected that Mrs. Sparling was poisoning her family, killing her husband and sons.

Since three Sparling men had mysteriously died, he was taken aback when Dr. MacGregor had approached him with his suspicions of arsenic poisoning and Carrie Sparling.

Dr. Conboy thought the conversation to be quite unusual and went to the county prosecuting attorney, Xenophon Boomhower.

The prosecutor, of course, was aware of the Sparling deaths. He had also been made aware of suspicions surrounding the deaths by the late John Sparling's uncle and namesake, John Sparling.

The older Sparling was concerned for the safety of the remaining two sons of his nephew and Carrie. He feared they might meet with the same excruciating death as their father and brothers.

Mr. Boomhower ordered that a nurse be hired to stay with Scyril to make sure he was not given anything that might harm him.

Dr. MacGregor made the arrangements and Nurse Gibbs was brought in from Port Huron.

The prosecutor shared the belief that Mrs. Sparling might be responsible for the deaths. He asked Dr. Conboy to go to the Sparling home and to try to frighten Mrs. Sparling into admitting her guilt in the poisoning.

When Dr. Conboy arrived at the Sparling house, he found Dr. MacGregor was already there. Dr. MacGregor was surprised, and agitated that Conboy was there.

Dr. Conboy told MacGregor his reason for the visit to throw a scare into the widow.

MacGregor told him not to waste his time that he himself had done it just that morning and he thought Mrs. Sparling was so fragile that she would need to be committed to an asylum within months.

Scyril's condition continued to deteriorate.

Prosecutor Boomhower ordered that if the young Sparling man should die from his infirmity, the county coroner would conduct a full postmortem. He wanted to once and for all get to the bottom of the cause of the Sparling deaths.

A few days later Scyril became the fourth of the Sparling men to die a mysterious death. He succumbed to the agonizing illness that wracked his body with excruciating pain.

Mr. Boomhower was notified by Dr. MacGregor of the boys passing. Boomhower said the county coroner would be at the farmhouse in the morning to perform the autopsy.

That evening, Dr. MacGregor asked Dr. Holdship to assist him in performing an autopsy on Scyril's body. The doctors did not find anything unusual, nothing that could definitely indicate a cause of death.

When the county corner, Dr. Morden, and Dr. Conboy arrived at the Sparling farm they were surprised to find the postmortem had already been completed.

Mr. Boomhower was angry that his orders were not followed and the county coroner did not perform the autopsy. He ordered the coroner and Dr. Conboy to carry out a second autopsy.

Scyril Sparling. From the Huron Daily Tribune, *Bad Axe, Michigan.*

In the second autopsy, the doctors found what they considered discrepancies. They removed several organs from Scyril's body and sent them to the forensic medicine laboratory of the University of Michigan in Ann Arbor.

The results from the University of Michigan arrived a few days later and changed the Huron County Prosecutors office from suspecting a crime might have occurred, to investigating the murder of Scyril Sparling.

The organs sent to the University of Michigan did not display signs of any disease but they did contain traces of arsenic, enough to easily kill a man. Boomhower had the evidence he needed to support his suspicions and ordered the body of Albert Sparling to be exhumed.

After an examination of Albert's organs, the laboratory at the University of Michigan determined Albert's cause of death to be the result of ingesting arsenic in fatal amounts.

John Sparling, the boy's father who had died over two years earlier and the second to die, Peter Sparling, were exhumed. Their remains were examined chemically and microscopically with the results showing no signs of disease that would result in death. The examination did reveal that both men had enough strychnine in their system to kill them. John, Peter, Albert and Scyril had all been poisoned. They were murdered.

All evidence pointed towards the widow Sparling. She had access to all of the dead men so she could have easily poisoned them. She had taken out an insurance policy on all of the dead men. She was the only one who would gain monetarily by their deaths. And Doctor MacGregor had told others that he suspected her of poisoning the family.

Sheriff McAuley of Huron County began to investigate the murders of the men. He followed Prosecutor Boomhower's suspicions and began to question the widow Sparling.

In the course of his interrogation, Sheriff McAuley learned that Carrie Sparling purchased $1,000 life insurance polices on each of her sons and she was the sole beneficiary of the policies. Further questioning revealed that the life insurance policies were purchased at the recommendation of Dr. MacGregor and purchased from the doctor's father's insurance company.

When asked what she had done with the money she was paid by the life insurance company she told Sheriff McAuley that she paid off farm debts, bought Dr. MacGregor an automobile and purchased the land and house Dr. and Mrs. MacGregor lived in.

It seemed to Sheriff McAuley that possibly Dr. MacGregor had a lot to gain from the insurance payments as well as Mrs. Sparling.

Doctors Herrington, Morden, and Conboy, who had all dealt with the Sparling men while they were ill or after their deaths were questioned by the sheriff. They all reported that at times Dr. MacGregor acted strange and made unusual statements to them about the Sparling men and their sickness and deaths.

During an examination of Scyril Sparling, Dr. MacGregor out of the blue, asked Dr. Conboy if he thought the boy had been poisoned. At another time the doctor hinted that he suspected all of the men had died as a result of poison, and the doctor told a reporter that he wasn't surprised that arsenic was found in the bodies of the men because they were all, the whole family, being treated for syphilis and the syphilis medication contained arsenic.

These statements led the sheriff to wonder if the good doctor might have more than a professional medical relationship with the Sparling family.

In a move that shocked the community, Sheriff McAuley arrested Dr. MacGregor for the murder of Scyril Sparling.

Due to the pre-trial publicity the case generated, the judge anticipated a huge crowd, and because of the dilapidated condition of the courthouse, Judge Beach ruled that the trial be moved to the second floor of the *Tribune* newspaper building.

As Judge Beach had suspected, the sensational trial would attract crowds like no other criminal trial in the history of the county. People lined the wooden staircase of the building with men and women straining to hear the proceedings. Others stood below on the walk and street listening to comments being relayed from those on the stairway.

A view of the rear of the Tribune building where the MacGregor trial was held. From the Bad Axe Historical Society.

During the nearly nine-week trial, it was brought out that the doctor had a financial relationship in the deaths of the Sparling men. He profited from the insurance policies on the men. He was bought an automobile and Mrs. Sparling purchased the home in which he and his wife lived.

Dr. and Mrs. MacGregor took their new automobile on a trip to the east. Mrs. Sparling gave money to the doctor for the trip and more money when they returned.

The hired hand of Dr. MacGregor testified that he had seen the doctor destroy several bottles of medicine after Albert Sparling died.

The doctor began to make statements that implicated Mrs. Sparling in the deaths. He said he thought she was responsible for poisoning her family. Mrs. Carrie Sparling was arrested soon after Dr. MacGregor for her part in the murders of her husband and sons.

The doctor told Sheriff McAuley that the four sons of John and Carrie Sparling had contracted syphilis and he was sure that the only remaining son, Ray would surely die from it as well. The doctor told the sheriff that John Sparling also died from the disease and that he had treated Mrs. Sparling for blindness on two occasions brought on from syphilis.

Annie Pieruski, a woman hired by Mrs. Sparling to help with meals and cleaning, testified that Dr. MacGregor made frequent visits to the farm. He often was there under the excuse of needing to treat Mrs. Sparling for an illness of the eye.

Annie told the court that when the doctor came, Mrs. Sparling would go into her bedroom. The doctor would join her in the bedroom and they would remain there behind the closed door for long periods of time.

While neither the doctor nor Mrs. Sparling admitted to having anything other than a strictly platonic, doctor patient relationship, the evidence begged to differ. The statement by Annie caused a commotion in the already sensational trial.

That a handsome doctor and the beautiful widow allegedly engaged in a torrent love affair resulting in the murder of her husband and three of her sons, was a story that newsmen drooled over. Newspapers from around the country picked up the intriguing story and followed the trial with daily updates.

The doctors that examined young Scyril Sparling, Dr. Holdship, Dr. Conboy, and Dr. Morden all testified about what they saw and heard, how they suspected the youngest Sparling had been poisoned but could not prove anything. They also told of strange comments that Dr. MacGregor made, comments that implicated himself and/or Mrs. Sparling.

After lengthy and eloquent closing statements by the prosecutor and defense attorneys, the jury retired to determine the future of Dr. Robert MacGregor.

On Friday June 7th, 1912 Judge Beach notified the attorneys that the jury had reached a verdict.

At 12:15, the foreman of the jury, Robert Bowman, rose and slowly read the verdict.

"We find Dr. Robert A. MacGregor guilty as charged of murder in the first degree of murdering Scyril Sparling by arsenical poisoning."

A week later, Dr. MacGregor was taken to the Tribune building to stand before Judge Beach for sentencing.

When asked if there was any reason sentencing should not be passed, Dr. MacGregor quietly responded: "Your honor, I am innocent. My case is in the hands of my attorneys. I leave it all to them."

The judge said he didn't want to lecture the defendant, he would only issue the sentence in accordance with law and the verdict delivered by the jury.

I sentence you, Robert MacGregor, to Jackson Prison for the remainder of your life for the murder of Scyril Sparling.

The proceeding took less than five minutes.

After the sensational trial that was covered across the country leading to the conviction of Dr. MacGregor, the furor seemed to quell. When Prosecutor Boomhower dismissed the charges against Mrs. Sparling for lack of evidence, it created a stir in the county but was hardly mentioned in the nationwide newspapers that earlier had followed the story.

THE HURON COUNTY TRIBUNE.

VOLUME XXXVII — BAD AXE, HURON COUNTY, MICHIGAN, FRIDAY, JUNE 7th, 1912 — NUMBER 23.

DR. MACGREGOR IS FOUND GUILTY

JURY GAVE VERDICT OF MURDER IN 1ST DEGREE

Said They Couldn't Do Anything Else With Evidence? First Vote Was 10 to 2 But Merely An Informal Ballot.

...CTOR NOT MUCH AFFECTED BY VERDICT AND TAKES SOUND SLEEP AFTERWARDS. SEEMED TO EXPECT IT.

Crime One of Most Appalling in State's History Much Sympathy for Stricken Family and Faithful Wife.

Prosecutor and Sheriff Get Much Praise for Their Part in Great Case. Sentence May be Given Next Monday and Will Be For Life.

Doctor MacGregor settled into life at Jackson Prison working as an assistant to the prison doctor and in the prison pharmacy.

The attorneys for Dr. MacGregor filed a petition for a new trial in 1912. They claimed a new witness came forward stating he had observed Scyril Sparling consuming large quantities of a patented tonic, advertised through newspapers and sold by traveling salesmen and in general stores. Judge Beach studied the new information and deliberated for weeks before deciding that the new information did not warrant a new trial.

The attorneys for the doctor took the appeal of the conviction and the life sentence to the Michigan Supreme Court. After consideration, the esteemed jurists of the highest court in the state upheld the decision of the lower court. Dr. Robert MacGregor's appeals had expired. As a last ditch effort, the doctor's attorneys wrote to Governor Ferris and appealed to the governor to pardon Dr. MacGregor.

In 1916, Governor Woodbridge N. Ferris decided to investigate the case of Dr. MacGregor.

Several witnesses were called before the governor's investigators. Residents of Ubly and the county seat of Bad Axe traveled to Lansing and others were interviewed in the county.

Governor Ferris called the Warden at Jackson Prison requesting that Dr. Robert MacGregor report to the capital in Lansing without delay and without prison guards. The Governor was convinced that Dr. MacGregor was innocent and after serving four years of a life sentence, the Governor granted him a full unconditional pardon.

When questioned as to what evidence the Governor discovered that had been missed by the jury of the original trial, the court of appeals and the Michigan Supreme Court, the Governor declined to say.

Dr. MacGregor was a free man and accepted an appointment as the Jackson Prison doctor and continued in this capacity until 1928 when he died of typhoid fever.

The case of the Sparling men dying in rural Michigan created a sensation in Michigan and across the nation as well. Reporters from Detroit were sent to follow the trial and their stories were related to newspapers in every major city of the nation. The crime contained all of the ingredients that the early 1900 populace yearned for in a true crime story; mystery, intrigue, murder, a good-looking doctor, a good-looking widow, and sex.

If the doctor wasn't guilty of the crimes, who was? It is a answer lost in history.

Its Not A Job, It Becomes An Obsession.

-University of Wisconsin Police Officer Lt. Gary Moore

Christine Rothschild was a beautiful 18-year-old student at the University of Wisconsin at Madison. The native of North Chicago, Illinois was a freshman at the University studying journalism and did modeling for department store catalogs during the summers. During the school year she lived in room 119 of Emery Hall on campus.

Around 7:00 pm on May 26, 1968, Phillip Van Valkenberg, a student at the University, was making his way through the bushes outside Sterling Hall to knock on a window, trying to get a friend's attention to let him in the building and out of the rain.

Behind the bushes, Phillip stumbled across the bloody dead body of Christine Rothschild.

The campus police swarmed the area searching for evidence that could help them identify the murderer.

An autopsy revealed that Christine was stabbed in the chest and neck at least 14 times. She also might have been strangled possibly with the liner of her coat. She was not sexually molested.

Wisconsin State Journal

WEATHER: Cloudy Today and Tonight. High Near 60, Low 45 to 50

GOOD MORNING

MADISON, TUESDAY MORNING, MAY 28, 1968 ★ ★ ★ MORNING FINAL 10°

NO SUSPECTS, MOTIVE SEEN IN UW SLAYING

Stabs, Blows
Disclosed
in Autopsy
By JUNE DIECKMANN

CHRISTINE ROTHSCHILD

'Why Her?' Friends Ask

A Happy Life Ends
for Well-Liked Girl

Despite the intense investigation by campus police, Madison Police and other law enforcement authorities, no suspects were established and no one was arrested. The police continued to search for the murderer but the trail had gone cold.

Not to minimize the murder of the beautiful freshman, but about a year after discovering Christine brutally murdered another violent crime struck the University of Wisconsin. The normally quiet campus was awakened at 3:20 am by an explosion.

Someone set off a bomb that blew a four-foot hole through the steel reinforced concrete floor of the Administrative building.

The building sustained $100,000 worth of damage but luckily no one was injured or killed.

No one was ever arrested for the bombing. No one or group claimed credit for the blast. No reason for the act of terrorism was uncovered.

The University was again the site of a bombing on August 24, 1970.

A van with six barrels of explosives was parked in a loading area of the University of Wisconsin Administration Building. The bomb was detonated injuring four and killing one researcher in the building.

The bombing was found to be the work of three men who were protesting the university's involvement in military research and development during the war in Vietnam.

The men were arrested and sentenced to prison.

On July 21, 1976, almost 8 years after the death of Christine Rothschild, another female body was discovered.

The burned and decomposed body of twenty year-old Debra Bennett was found by a land surveying crew, it had been dumped in a gully along Old Sauk Pass Road, about 14 miles from Madison in western Dane County.

An autopsy, performed by Dr. Billy Bauman, could not determine the cause of death but he was able to conclude Debra had been dead for at least 10 days. Dental records were necessary to identify that the charred corpse was that of Debra Bennett.

Debra was from Ridgeway, Iowa and had moved to Madison only a short time before, to escape the small town and experience the college atmosphere Madison offered. She worked as a waitress and had recently been evicted from her apartment.

She was last seen walking barefoot along Loftsgordon Avenue away from the apartment. She was going to be staying at the Cardinal Hotel in the downtown area.

Police Seek Clues in Death of Debra Bennett

'Big City' Wasn't Answer for Small Town Girl

By FLOYD NELSON JR
© The Leader Times Stat

Debra Bennett

Oddly, the Cardinal Hotel key given to Debra was mailed back to the hotel three weeks after she was found dead. There was no note, no return address or any identifying marks.

Two years later on June 21, 1978 a farmer walking along a wooded path near Woodland Road west of Waunakee discovered a woman's nude body partially buried in a shallow grave. The woman, who died of blunt force trauma to the head, had been dead an estimated three weeks.

The body was so decayed it took two days to identify the woman as 18 year-old Julie Ann Hall.

Julie had moved to Madison from the small town of North Freedom, Wisconsin and hoped the move would offer the turn around she desperately needed.

She obtained a job on the University of Wisconsin campus as a library assistant.

On the night she disappeared, Julie was seen at a local pub.

Early in the investigation, the police felt confident that they had a strong suspect in the murder of Julie Hall but as time passed the suspect proved to be innocent of the crime.

Another female disappeared from the Madison area on March 27, 1979.

Julie Speerschneider worked at the Red Caboose Day Care Center in Madison. The well-liked twenty year-old was last seen at the 602 Club located on University Avenue. She was ready to leave and decided to hitchhike home.

After she disappeared, a man reading the newspaper recognized Julie as a hitchhiker he had given a ride to. The man called the police and informed them that he had dropped Julie and an unidentified male companion off at the corner of Johnson and Brearly.

A reward was offered and the family consulted a psychic but with little evidence for the police to go on, the disappearance of Julie Speerschneider went cold.

State

Wisconsin State Journal   Saturday, May 2, 1981, Section 4

Brucellosis traced	Column 5
Death notices	Page 2
Want ads	Page 3

Four dead, and police 'waiting for a break'

Julie Ann Hall   Julie Speerschneider   Sue LeMahieu   Debra J. Bennett

Susan LeMahieu, a twenty-four year-old young woman went missing on December 15, 1979. Susan was mildly mentally impaired and slightly handicapped and was known as a street person.

At first the police assumed she had simply wandered off, until her body was discovered lying in greenery near the University of Wisconsin Arboretum.

Susan LeMahieu died of multiple stab wounds to her chest.

The police had developed two strong suspects but each was cleared of involvement in Susan's death.

The murder of another Madison young woman was void of evidence and the case, like the others went cold.

In April of 1981, a hiker walking along the Yahara River in the town of Dunn, Wisconsin discovered the badly decomposed body of Julie Speerschneider.

The remains of Julie who went missing on March 27, 1979, was mostly skeletal and partially covered by brush. A cause of death could not be determined due to the extreme decomposition.

Just months after the discovery of Julie Speerschneider, in July 1981, the decomposed body of Shirley Stewart was found in a wooded area north of Madison in the town of Westport, Wisconsin.

Ms. Stewart was missing since January 2, 1980 when she was seen leaving her job at the Dean Clinic.

Shirley Stewart's body was in such a bad state of decomposition that the pathologist was unable to establish a cause of death.

Donna Mraz, a nineteen year-old beauty, was the next to die a violent death.

Donna was a waitress and was last seen on her way home from work.

Camp Randall Stadium, home of the University of Wisconsin Badgers football team, on the Madison campus was the location of the murder of Donna Mraz, she had been stabbed repeatedly.

Robbery was not a motive, Donna's money and paycheck were still in her possession and she was not sexually molested.

There was little evidence found to assist the police in solving the murder of Donna Mraz. Her case, as with the others went unsolved.

On November 17, 1984 deer hunters found the decaying body of a young woman. The autopsy revealed that the remains were that of a missing University of Wisconsin student, Janet Raasch.

Ms. Raasch, a business major in the third year of her studies, was last seen on October 11, 1984. Friends reported her missing four days later on October 15.

The investigation uncovered that a friend had dropped her off on Highway 54 in the town of Buena Vista, Wisconsin. She was found just two miles from where she was dropped off.

The autopsy could not determine a cause of death due to the severe decomposition of the body.

All of the deaths of the young women were tragic in their own right but the number of deaths going unsolved was astounding.

Over the course of more than sixteen years, young women were tragically and violently murdered. There were some similarities between the deaths; the girls all had some relationship to the University of Wisconsin, as students or employees, they lived on or near campus or socialized with students of the university.

Each was young and wore their hair long and parted in the same way and they were all found murdered just a short distance from Wisconsin's capitol city of Madison.

However, to this day it is still unknown if the same person or persons are responsible for all of the deaths.

Wisconsin State Journal

Saturday

July 3, 1982
Madison, Wisconsin
30 pages ★★★ 30 cents

Few leads in murder

Donna Mraz

None of the killings were solved, no one was arrested, no one was brought to justice.

The murders have stopped yet it is unknown if the murderer continued to kill but changed his way of disposing of the bodies. Possibly the murderer was imprisoned for an unrelated crime, or moved to another part of the country. Or possibly he died.

The deaths of the girls now between 28 and 44 years ago remain open with the police agencies. If anyone has information that might assist the police in bringing the investigation into the deaths of the young women to a close, they are asked to contact the University of Wisconsin Campus Police, the Madison Police department or the Dane County Sheriff's Department.

The Death Of Sharin' Morningstar Keenan

On Sunday, January 23, 1983, nine year-old Sharin' and her mother spent the day in Toronto, Canada. On the way home she begged her mother to let her go to the park near their house to play a bit before nightfall. Lynda, Sharin's mother agreed but told her to be home by 4:30.

Sometime between 3:00 and 3:30, Sharin', a fourth grader at Ketchum School, went off to the Jean Sibelius Park near her Dupont Street home.

Sharin's father, Caron, walked to the park to get his daughter but she was not anywhere to be found. Thinking that possibly she had walked home and arrived in his absence he returned home. On his arrival he learned that Sharin' was not there either.

Sharin' was not the type of child to wander off without telling her parents where she was going, Lynda and Caron Keenan became concerned. They searched the neighborhood around their home and the park looking for their pretty daughter with long dark brown hair.

Not finding any sign of their daughter, the Keenan's called the police.

The police began a search of the neighborhood that evening and a missing person report was broadcast on the police frequency to all emergency vehicles.

Sharin' was still not found by the following day and the

Nine year old Sharin' Morningstar Keenan disappeared on January 23, 1983.

police set up surveillance equipment in case the disappearance was a kidnapping and the person responsible might call. A call never came.

The police searched the area within a 10-block radius of Jean Sibelius Park and used a sound truck to drive through the neighborhood announcing news of the missing child and asking for anyone with knowledge of the missing child to come forward.

A neighborhood man, Doug Baptie, reported to the police that he was walking home on Sunday about 4:00 PM and observed a young girl answering the description of Sharin' Keenan in the park. She was standing on the ice rink talking to a man. The man was smoking and standing just off the rink.

Baptie thought it was unusual that the two would be standing in the park talking while a light rain fell. The girl looked at Baptie, making eye contact. Baptie continued walking but turned around to see the young girl and older man leaving the park, walking north on Brunswick Avenue.

Doug Baptie described the man as 5'-9"/10" tall and weighing about 160-180 pounds. From his description the police artist made a sketch of the man seen talking with Sharin'. The sketch was distributed throughout the neighborhood.

Based on Baptie's statement the police concentrated their search on houses closer to the park.

On February 1, 1983, nine days after Sharin' Morningstar Keenan went to the park and disappeared, her body was found crammed in a refrigerator of a second floor apartment in a rooming house on Brunswick Ave.

The pretty nine-year-old girl had been sexually molested then strangled and stuffed in the working refrigerator.

The person, who rented the apartment, Michael Robert Burns, had not been seen since the day after the young girl went missing.

The police learned that Michael Burns was a false identity and the investigation intensified resulting with the police on March 5, 1983 naming Dennis Melvyn Howe as a suspect in the rape and strangulation murder of Sharin' Keenan.

Howe was born in Regina and before moving to Toronto served over 20 years in prison on charges of armed robbery, unlawful confinement and sexual assault.

In 1969 he abducted a woman as she got into her car and forced her to drive 160 miles north to Saskatoon then another 60 miles southeast to

A photograph of Dennis Melvyn Howe as he appeared in the early 1970s.

Davidson, where he robbed her at knifepoint and assaulted her. After 11 ½ hours she was able to escape.

He was released from prison on February 17, 1982 at Prince Albert, under the stipulation that he remain under supervision. Three days later, he left town and disappeared.

At the time of the murder, Dennis Melvyn Howe was described as five feet nine inches and about 165 pounds. He is left handed with thinning brown hair that is graying at the sides. He has brown eyes and a tanned weathered complexion. He is known to have badly rotting teeth which cause him much pain and he can easily be identified by a gap between his front teeth, a scar under his chin and a crooked little finger.

Those that knew him say he has a hairy chest and arms and is a loud and boisterous individual who often calls people and things, "Turkey."

In the past he has worked as a cook, janitor, millwright, electrician, carpenter and metal worker and has gone by the aliases; Wayne King, Ralph Ferguson, and Jim Meyers.

At the time of the murder of the young girl in Toronto, Howe wore a mustache and was known as a heavy smoker with a hearty deep laugh.

The Canadian law enforcement authorities, in June 1984, started a countrywide campaign looking for Dennis Howe and offering a $100,000 reward for information resulting in the arrest of the murderer.

Dennis Howe was last seen at a bus station in Sault Saint Marie, Ontario. His current location is unknown. Tips have said he may be living in Canada, United States or Mexico.

Every few years, the police develop an age enhanced sketch of what Dennis Howe would look like at the time, but in the 40 years that have passed, Dennis Howe has not been found. He may be dead or he may still be alive and preying on other young innocent victims.

If anyone can be of assistance in locating Dennis Howe they are asked to immediately call the sheriff or police department where they are located.

Author's Note: This chapter is different from the others in this book in that the murderers have not been identified. In the murder and rape of Sharin' Keenan the police have a very strong suspect but are unable to find him. The Police seek the assistance of the public in finding Dennis Melvyn Howe.

Cyanide Will Kill You

....

Life was so much simpler in 1982. Computers, only used on college campuses and large corporations were soon to become a household word with the release of the Commodore 64. Gasoline was only .91 cents per gallon meaning you could buy a muscle car without a thought of miles per gallon or environmental damage. You could get the weather forecast just by turning on a new cable TV network called The Weather Channel, we listened to the biggest selling record of all time, *Thriller*, by Michael Jackson, we didn't have to push 1 for English, and we could open over the counter medications by just turning the top; there was no tamper resistant packaging.

But, not everything was ideal in 1982. Air Florida flight 90 crashed into the Potomac River in Washington D.C. killing 78 people, Wayne Williams, dubbed the Atlanta Child Murderer, was convicted, Britain and Argentina went to war over the Falkland Islands. But life in 1982 was about to become scary and much more complicated and forever change the way we live.

In September 29, 1982 in Elk Grove Village, a suburb of Chicago, a twelve-year-old girl woke up her parents in the early morning hours complaining of a sore throat and other cold symptoms. To help her feel better and get the sleep she needed to fight off the cold, she was given one Tylenol® capsule.

At 7:00 AM that morning, her parents found her unconscious on the floor of the bathroom. The girl was rushed to the hospital where she later died. The doctors suspected she had suffered a stroke.

The Chicago metropolitan area, or "Chicagoland," as it is often referred to, in the 1980s had a combined population of almost 9 million people and encompassed hundreds of square miles. On the 29th day of September, 1982, as in any normal day in a large city and suburbs, many people were taken to area hospitals for various problems. When paramedics were called to the Arlington Heights home of 27-year-old Adam Janus, no one suspected there was a connection between him and the twelve year old who died in another hospital earlier that day.

After attempts to save Adam, a postal worker, he succumbed to what the doctors believed was a massive heart attack. They would know more after the autopsy.

Cyanide is deadly but easy to get

During the funeral of his brother, Stanley Janus from Lisle, Illinois was understandably distraught by the unexpected death. Stan and his wife Theresa complained of headaches, probably brought on by the stress of the days past, and took Tylenol® capsules to relieve the pain.

Shortly thereafter, the young couple, ages 25 and 19 collapsed to the floor, later in the hospital they were both declared dead.

Three deaths in one family was suspicious and the hospital notified the police.

Two firemen were discussing the death of the young girl in Elk Grove Village. They also had known about Adam Janus's death and heard he had ingested a Tylenol® previous to being found unconscious. They called paramedics who treated Stan and Theresa Janus and discovered they too had taken Tylenol® prior to their deaths and the connection between four seemingly unrelated deaths had been established.

The police immediately went to the home of the victims and took the bottles of Tylenol® for forensic testing. The capsules in the Tylenol® bottles were found to contain 65 milligrams of potassium cyanide.

A person who ingests cyanide becomes red in the face due to the oxygen in the bloodstream being depleted by the poison, breathing becomes labored and the person slips from consciousness, sometimes with convulsions, then the person dies.

The poison has been used by religious cults, such as Jim Jones's People Temple and San Diego's Heavens Gate to commit mass suicide and by members of the Nazi Party to end their lives at the end of the World War II.

Once the connection of deaths of people who had taken Tylenol® capsules was established, the manufacturer of the capsules, McNeil Consumer Healthcare, a subsidiary of Johnson & Johnson, was alerted and they immediately started a recall of the pain reliever.

Store shelves were emptied and the Tylenol® checked, several more bottles were found to have been tampered with and contained cyanide, unfortunately, not before three more people died from cyanide poisoning. All of the deaths occurred in the greater Chicago area.

A nationwide recall of Tylenol® products resulted in an estimated 31 million bottles being recalled at a retail value exceeding $100,000,000.

Someone had emptied Tylenol® Extra Strength capsules of their medication and replaced it with the cyanide. At first it was suspected it had been done in the manufacturing process. But the tainted bottles had been produced in different locations. Rather, police theorize a person visited several Chicago area stores, purchased bottles of the pain reliever, replaced the medication with the poison then replaced the bottles back on the store shelves, where unsuspecting people bought them, took them, and died.

The newspapers announced the news to the public that seven people had been killed by over the counter drugs that had been tampered with resulted in public outrage.

People never bothered to think about the safety of over the counter drugs or for that matter anything they purchased for consumption. When people started dying the public felt betrayed, their trust was gone. A criminal could poison anything, from over the counter medication to a bag of jellybeans.

Panic ensued.

Law enforcement authorities from all levels worked around the clock to find the sick and depraved person responsible for the random murders of the seven people who all lived in either Cook or DuPage counties.

One path the investigation took was to look at spouses and others close to the victims. Did they have a reason to kill the victim? Could they have been so cold hearted to intentionally kill innocent people to cover their crime? Some of the murders appeared suspicious but were soon dismissed.

Tainted Tylenol® Extra Strength capsules killed people other than the original seven, but upon investigation authorities discovered they were copycat crimes; a family member used the original crime to try and cover up their own murder. It didn't work and they were arrested.

> *Tylenol task force sifting through thousands of tips*

Investigators have 'principal suspects' in cyanide manhunt

Calif. strychnine caps considered unrelated

A break in the case came when Johnson & Johnson received a letter informing them the Tylenol® murders would cease if the company paid one million dollars.

On December 13, 1982 the F.B.I. arrested James W. Lewis for extortion.

It was found that Lewis had written the letter to Johnson & Johnson and he also was guilty of writing a letter to the White House demanding President Reagan change his policies related to taxes or the writer would blow up the White House and the Tylenol® killings would continue.

Handwriting analysis verified that Lewis had written the letters but during the time of the poisoning James Lewis was living in New York City with his wife.

Lewis was convicted of attempted extortion but not for the Tylenol® murders in the Chicago area. He was sentenced to 20 years in prison and released on parole after serving 12 years.

There were other persons of interest in the poisoning of the seven Chicago area people but after intense investigation they were released.

The investigators working the Tylenol® murders pursued all avenues to determine the identity of the perpetrator. Ted Kaczynski, the "Unabomber" was also listed as a suspect.

Ted Kaczynski, is currently serving life in prison for killing three people and injuring more than twenty others with mail bombs.

Kaczynski was a native of Evergreen Park, a Chicago suburb, where he began exploding bombs. Two bombs attributed to Kaczynski were detonated at Chicago's Northwestern University and another bomb was found on a commercial airliner leaving the city's O'Hare Airport.

Kaczynski provided a DNA sample but the authorities have yet to disclose if he had any involvement in the murders.

Yet another theory of the identity of the Tylenol® Murderer was presented in the 2011 book, *The Tylenol® Mafia*. Author Scott Bartz stated that the person responsible for the seven tainted Tylenol® deaths in Chicago was a Johnson & Johnson employee who was dissatisfied with the company and replaced extra strenth capsules with capsules filled with cyanide. The person did it in a Johnson & Johnson distribution center rather than at the retail level as was suspected.

Bartz further suggests that Johnson & Johnson knew about it and chose to keep quiet to avoid liability.

No further evidence has been discovered to confirm the authors account.

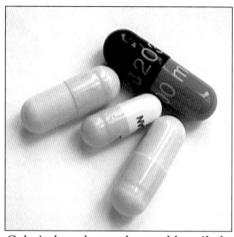

The tragic Tylenol® murders of 1982 in the Chicago Metropolitan Area resulted in changes to the packaging of many products. All over the

Gelatin based capsules could easily be taken apart and refilled with another substance. Photograph from Wikipedia Commons.

counter drugs must now be packaged in a tamper resistant container that once opened looks obviously like it has been opened and alerts the purchaser not to purchase it.

Another change that occurred based on the distribution of the tainted capsules in 1982 was the elimination of drugs being sold in capsule form. It was simply too easy to pull the two halves apart, pour out the medication and replace it with some foreign material. Tylenol® and other medications now come in solid caplets, pills in the shape of a capsule. Capsules are no longer available.

No one has been convicted of the murder of the seven victims of the Tylenol® murderer. In the three decades since, citizens around the nation and the world lost trust in products manufactured for their consumption and a time of innocence was forever dismissed, the sick murderer who randomly killed unsuspecting people was never brought to justice.

A Murder Case Is Open Forever

Murder is often thought of as a crime of large urban areas, but unfortunately small cities and towns are not immune to the horrific crime, they sometimes fall victim at the hands of killers.

Marquette, Michigan is a small city located in Michigan's Upper Peninsula. French missionaries visiting the area early in the 17th century found the wilderness of the area plentiful in animals which attracted the French fur trappers in the 19th century. And the natural harbor at Marquette made it a good stopping point for vessels traveling on Lake Superior.

The discovery of iron deposits west of Marquette in 1844 created a boom with mines opening to reap the harvest of the earth's treasures.

Marquette was first organized as a village in 1849 with the name New Worcester but a year later it was re-named Marquette in honor of Father Jacques Marquette the French Jesuit missionary who had explored the area.

The iron and copper found in abundant supply brought wealthy businessmen to build mines and miners in large numbers. Many of the miners were recent immigrants to the country from all around the world, many from Norway and Sweden.

Railroads were built from the mines to Marquette to haul the iron ore to sailing ships anchored in the harbor. As sail gave way to steam and ships became larger, an ore dock was built in Marquette Harbor.

Ore laden railroad cars were pushed up onto the ore dock, their bottoms opened and the ore dropped into bins below the track.

A ship would tie up along side the dock, a chute lowered and the ore slid down the chutes into the ship's cargo hold. Loading ships much faster with an ore dock, taking hours rather than the days it took with the previous methods.

The large Great Lake freighters are still a frequent visitor to Marquette, bringing in coal for the generating plant and taking loads of iron ore to the steel mills in the lower lakes.

Some of the mines are now closed, only the most productive remaining in operation, lumbering the vast virgin pine forests that was once a major source of employment is still a viable occupation on a much smaller scale, but the city still prospers.

The city's population swells each fall as thousands of college students move to town to attend Northern Michigan University. Many of the students, as do most visitors, grow an attachment to Marquette and the serene peacefulness that is the Upper Peninsula.

The quiet peacefulness of Marquette was interrupted when Erin Rebecca Taylor, a secretary at the Upper Peninsula Medical Center in Marquette went missing.

Erin, twenty-four years old, was not originally from the Upper Peninsula town; rather she was from the Wisconsin capitol of Madison and had moved to Marquette in 1999 with a friend and her friend's family.

Well liked and described by co-workers as very nice and caring, Erin was single and lived by herself in a small rental home on Wright Street in Marquette.

Like many singles, Erin, became involved in the online dating phenomena. She met and conversed via email with various men eventually becoming close to a man from South Carolina and another from Windsor, Ontario.

The Internet relationship with the Windsor man grew to the point they wanted to meet. Plans were made for the man to drive from his Windsor home to Munising, Michigan on August 11, 2000 where he and Erin arranged to meet at a hotel. As a precaution, Erin told friends and co-workers she was meeting the man and where before she drove the approximate 40 miles from Marquette to Munising.

The Canadian man arrived at the hotel as scheduled, however he had not made reservations and found there were no rooms available. He was not able to contact Erin to tell her of the change of plans so he remained at the hotel waiting for Erin to arrive. But Erin did not arrive.

Thinking that something had delayed her, the Canadian man waited, but after hours had passed and still Erin had not arrived he drove to Marquette to look for her.

He checked her home and other obvious locations where he thought he might find Erin but he couldn't find her anywhere. Probably out of a feeling of rejection he gave up and drove back to Windsor.

Erin did not show up at work the following Monday morning. Friends and co-workers who knew of her meeting with a man she had met online noticed her absence. They were concerned but not worried, possibly she was enjoying her time with the man and had decided to spend more time with him.

A friend of Erin's, a local man, from the Marquette area, was concerned that he could not get in touch with her. He had tried to reach her for days to no avail. On Tuesday August 15[th,] out of concern for Erin's well being, he contacted the police.

The authorities took a statement from the man who told the police about Erin's practice of online dating and about her meeting a Canadian man in a hotel in Munising.

At that time there was no evidence that Erin had been abducted or had just gone on an impromptu vacation, but the Canadian man was listed as a person of interest in the possible disappearance of Erin Rebecca Taylor.

The police located the Windsor man and interviewed him at length. He willingly told them he had made arrangements to meet Erin at a motel in Munising but that she had not shown up. He told the police he had driven to Marquette looking for her but had not found her.

The police took the man's statement and he was listed as a suspect.

The disappearance of Erin remained a mystery.

Weather(Details On Page 5A)

80 75 75

Marquette, Michigan

THE MINING Journal

THE UPPER PENINSULA'S LARGEST DAILY NEWSPAPER

50 cents

Body found may be missing woman

By JAMES LAKE

Marquette County, in fact the entire Upper Peninsula, is blessed with natures beauty; vast tracts of hard and softwood forests, rivers, waterfalls, eagles, bear, deer and other woodland creatures abound. Local residents and thousands of visitors partake in snowmobiling on groomed trails through the woods that often follow old logging trails or deserted railroad right-of-way. The rest of the year the snowmobiles are put in storage and motorcycles and 4 wheel-drive off-road recreational vehicles explore the trails.

On August 20, 2000, Deputy David Derocher, of the Marquette County Sheriff's Department was investigating a complaint about off road vehicles abusing the trails.

While walking "Snowmobile Trail 8," one and a half miles east of the intersection of M-35 and County Road 492 he noticed a pile of what appeared to be trash about twelve feet off the trail. The litter turned out to be articles of bedding. As he investigated further, the deputy discovered under the bedding a decomposed body.

The body was laying face down and covered with a blanket. The partially clothed deceased had long brown hair, painted fingernails and pierced ears. The investigators found some personal items, suspected to belong to the deceased, folded under the body. However the body was so decomposed it was impossible to identify whether the body was that of a woman or a man. Also from its advanced state of decay the police could not tell if the person had died of natural causes, had died of a self inflicted wound or had died at the hands of another.

Law enforcement officials from the Marquette County Sheriff's Department and the Michigan State Police Crime Lab in Marquette scoured the area searching for any bits of evidence that might have been left behind. The body was badly decomposed and it couldn't be determined if the body was the missing Erin Taylor.

Randy Smith, the Marquette County Medical Examiner, after a forensic examination of the body determined the remains were that of a female and that she had died of un-natural causes. He was able to detect ligature marks on her neck proving the woman had been strangled.

However, dental records from Madison, Wisconsin were needed to verify if the body was that of the Marquette woman who had been missing for nine days.

A few days later the city's newspaper, the *Marquette Mining Journal*, reported in bold print that the body found in the woods off of County Road 492 was indeed that of Erin Rebecca Taylor.

The Marquette Sheriff's Department, the Marquette Police Department, the Marquette County Sheriff's Department and the Michigan State Police combined to investigate the death of the 24-year-old.

Since Erin had been reported missing, the primary suspect had been the man she had befriended on the Internet, the man from Windsor, Ontario.

Perhaps the man had misrepresented himself to Erin and rather than the nice guy she thought he was, he was a deranged pervert that used the internet to meet women online, convince them to meet him and then he would enact his sadistic criminal desires on them.

The crime lab technicians made a thorough search of Erin's house at the corner of Wright Street at Woodland Avenue. Evidence at the house showed she had been killed in the house on August 11, 2000 sometime after 10:00 PM. Her body was then transported by the perpetrator and dumped near the "Snowmobile Trail."

But after several interviews with the Canadian man and the lie detector examination the man readily agreed to take, the Windsor, Ontario man who met Erin online was cleared of any involvement in her disappearance.

Erin's computer, taken in as evidence, revealed other men whom she had been in communication with and they were interrogated. The police also interviewed dozens of people who may have information about Erin's disappearance. The police developed a list of 15 people whom were considered potential suspects. One by one they were eliminated.

About two weeks into the investigation the police brought in some fresh eyes to take a look at the case. Michigan State Police Trace Evidence technicians and a behavioral scientist from the Violent Crimes Unit traveled to Marquette from Lansing.

The behavioral scientist explained in a newspaper article that a lab processes physical evidence, but a behavioral scientist looks at what the evidence says about the killer. Some call it profiling.

They determined that the killer was someone that Erin Taylor knew, she apparently had let the person or persons into her house. They also reinforced the idea that the killer was a local person, someone who was familiar with the area where the body was dumped.

As the investigation continued all but one suspect was cleared of any involvement... the man who originally called the police to report Erin missing became the prime suspect in her disappearance and death.

Authorities suspect he could be the person who killed Erin Taylor. He had been romantically involved with Erin at one time. He was familiar with her home and also had intimate knowledge of the snowmobile trails in the Marquette area.

The police have not publicly identified the man, but say he is a married man around the age of Erin who admits to being close to her and lives in the area.

In the years since August 11, 2000, the person responsible for the death of the vivacious 24 year-old woman has not been identified.

Detective Gordon Warchock of the Marquette City Police is still seeking evidence in the murder of Erin Taylor. As new methods of forensic technology evolve, the evidence is reviewed.

The case of the murder of Erin Taylor remains open and unsolved, but as Detective Warchock says "A murder case is open forever." And the case will not be closed until the person responsible for the death of Erin Taylor is brought to justice. To report information on the Taylor murder case, call the Marquette City Police Department at 906- 228-0400.

How Could Anyone Be So Cruel As To Kill My Little Girl?

Ray Peter's day started off like most of his other days, but Friday, March 4, 1938 was going to be a day that would remain imprinted in his mind and haunt him for the rest of his life.

Mr. Peters operated a shoe store and shoe repair business on Jefferson Avenue SE in Grand Rapids, Michigan. Twelve years at the same location, he would boast.

On that Friday, he had errands to run. His father-in-law dropped him off at the license bureau to get plates for his car, and he needed a roll of sandpaper for one of his shoe repair machines.

As he walked to the abrasive supply company to get the sandpaper, he noticed they were frying perch in the window of the Kresge 5 & 10 store and stopped in for a plateful for lunch.

Ray Peters, the shoe repairman who discovered the bloody body in the stockroom. Courtesy of Philip Morton, True Crime Library.

After lunch, Mr. Peters walked to the Judd Building on Ionia Avenue, climbed the three flights of stairs to the Behr-Manning office and stockroom to purchase the sandpaper.

From the stairway he walked to the office. Finding no one in the office he started to walk back towards the stairs thinking it odd there was no one in the office, after all it was 1:25, they should be back from lunch by now. His thought was

The interior of the Behr-Manning Abrasive Supply Company. Courtesy of Philip Morton, True Crime Library.

disrupted when he heard a noise coming from the abrasive material stacked in aisles in the stockroom.

It sounded almost like a groan or a moan.

He opened the door to the stockroom, walked the main aisle looking down each row of neatly stacked abrasive supplies. He stopped in shock when about 40 feet down an aisle he saw a person on the floor lying across the walkway.

He slowly approached the prone figure. It was a woman lying on her back, her head and face crimson with blood.

He ran from the stockroom to the stairs and raced to the ground floor and out to the street. Seeing no one he went inside to the Manufacturers Supply Company on the first floor, seeking help.

There, the visibly shaken Peters, found some men engaged in a card game. Peters excitedly told the men of the injured girl on the third floor.

Arthur Leopold telephoned for an ambulance, and then joined Calvin DeBlaey, both employed by the Manufacturers Supply Company, at the freight elevator at the back of the building and ascended to the third floor, while Peters ran up the stairway. The men knelt over the slender prone body of the frail young woman, her head lying in a pool of blood. Leopold pulled out a handkerchief and wiped blood from the unconscious girl's lips as she quietly moaned in obvious pain.

Leopold went to the street to direct the ambulance personnel to the victim. The other two men stayed with the young woman who was barely holding to life.

Otto Reinsma and Charles Hilary, police officers and also ambulance attendants, raced through Grand Rapids in their ambulance to the Judd Building. They were met by Leopold who guided them up the two flights of stairs.

They knelt next to the body, evaluating her condition. The woman was about 19 or 20 years old, was still breathing but very labored. She wore a black dress with white collar and cuffs, nylon stockings and pumps. She had been struck several times about the head with some object. Her hair was caked with coagulating blood.

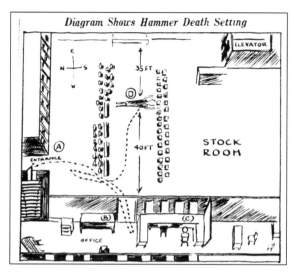

Diagram Shows Hammer Death Setting

The two officers administered first aid, placed the limp body of the young woman on a stretcher and quickly drove, with siren wailing and lights flashing, to Saint Mary's Hospital. Taylor and Frank Breen, searched the stockroom and offices of the Behr-Manning Company. A pencil lay near where the girl's body had. They also discovered a small fragment on the floor. She had been so severely beaten that a piece of her skull was knocked out of her head.

Boxes of abrasive supplies near the location where Peters found the girl, showed signs of dried blood splattered three feet off the floor indicating the girl was beaten as she lay injured on the wood floor of the stockroom. There was no blood splatter found between the girl's desk and where she was found, indicating she was not beaten in another location and dragged to the stockroom. The assault occurred where she lay.

Peters said her clothing was not disarranged as if to suggest she was sexually assaulted.

The police searched for the instrument that might have been used to severely pummel the young woman. From the appearance of the wounds on her skull, a hammer or such type of tool may have been used to beat the girl.

Not finding the weapon in the Behr-Manning office or stockroom, they searched the entire building; the Manufacturers Supply Company that occupied the ground floor and the second and fourth floors that did not have tenants at the time. Nothing that looked like it could inflict the damaging wounds was found.

Three hours after arriving at the hospital the young woman who was found so brutally beaten about the head died of the injuries, never regaining consciousness.

Dr. Simon LeRoy told the police that he was certain the girl had not sustained the injuries in a fall; rather she had sustained five blows to the head with a hammer like tool. She had been murdered!

Three blows were on the left side of her head; one in back of her left ear, one in front of the left ear and the third just to the left of the base of the skull. Two other blows were found on the right side of her head, one in front of the right ear and one just behind the right ear. The only other injury found was a broken right little finger, an apparent defensive wound sustained while the girl attempted to block the attack.

The woman's purse, located near her desk was searched. The authorities found her identification and a piece of paper with the following written; "May I give you just a few words of advice? Please don't hurt the next girl you love."

The words written in pencil were crossed out and below was written; "May I give you just a few words of advice? Please be a little more considerate with the next girl you fall in love with."

The owner of Behr-Manning, Charles O. Blackford and his son, Robert, just a few years older than the dead girl, returned to the Judd building as

Detectives Anning Taylor, left and Frank Breen (right) of the Grand Rapids Police Department. Courtesy of Philip Morton, True Crime Library.

THE WEATHER

The Grand Rapids Herald
HOME EDITION

GRAND RAPIDS, MICH., SATURDAY, MARCH 5, 1938

GRAND RAPIDS GIRL DIES AFTER BRUTAL ATTACK IN OFFICE; NO CLUE TO KILLER

Stenographer Beaten to Death

Mina Dekker Is Murder Victim

Stenographer's Skull Fractur 1 5
Times by Assailant's Blows

Cobbler Distraught Over
Finding Slain Girl's Body

the police were searching the building. They told the police the young woman was Mina Dekker, stenographer for the Behr-Manning Abrasive Supply Corporation.

She had worked for the Blackford's since she graduated from business school.

When told of her daughter's death, Mrs. Dekker sobbed, "How could anyone be so cruel as to kill my little girl? Just this morning she kissed me good-bye and went to work so happily, and now I'll never see her again."

Miss Dekker was a well-liked, pretty 19-year-old girl living with her parents, sister Maria and brother Adrian.

After graduating South High School in 1936 she attended a business college and was working at her first job at Behr-Manning.

She was known for her voice, having been a member of the South Glee Club and the choir at her church, the Fifth Reform Church.

Her family was at a loss for a reason for someone to savagely beat their daughter to death. She had no enemies; everyone liked her, who would want to do her harm?

During the interview with the family of Mina Dekker the detectives learned that the murdered girl had recently broken up with a boy she had once intended to marry.

Mina's sister, Maria Dekker, four years older than the murdered girl told police that she and her sister were very close and confided everything with one another. She talked of the break up of Mina and her boyfriend. How they intended to get married but Mina found out that he had gone out with another girl and Mina had broken off the relationship.

John Schafer, a nineteen-year-old student, was interviewed and admitted that he had been Mina's steady for a while and they had intended to marry when they had enough money. But the relationship became strained since he went out with another girl. The young man obviously emotionally distraught at the news of savage murder of his girlfriend, told the police that he was confident that they would have made up and married.

John Schafer told police that he had seen Mina the day of the murder during her lunch hour. He wanted to talk to her about making amends and getting back together.

The police considered him a suspect. He had motive; the failed

Mina Dekker, the stenographer who was viciously murdered in the abrasives company stockroom. Courtesy of Philip Morton, True Crime Library.

relationship, and opportunity; he was with the victim before she was killed.

He told the police that after seeing Mina he went back to the business college where he was taking classes. Several students and faculty verified that he returned to the college about 12:30 and was seen there for the next three hours. His alibi checked out, he was eliminated as a suspect, just a grieving boyfriend.

The police questioned Charles O. Blackford and his son Robert. They were both at the Behr-Manning office just prior to the girl being viciously murdered.

The men checked the office to see if anything had been stolen. The small amount of cash left in the office was still there and nothing looked to be disturbed.

The senior Blackford told Detectives Taylor and Breen that Mina had taken her lunch from 11:30 until 12:30. When Miss Dekker returned, he and his son left for lunch about 12:40. The police checked with the Pantlind Hotel where they said they had dined. The wait staff verified the men had dined there.

Mr. Blackford said he had gone to a store after lunch to purchase a suit. The personnel at the haberdashery agreed that the senior Blackford had been at the store and had purchased a suit during the time period the police theorized Mina was heinously murdered. He was not a suspect.

Robert Blackford, the owner's young good looking son had left his father after they had lunch. The police wondered; had he gone back to the business to spend some private time with the pretty stenographer? Had he forced his attention on the young girl just a year out of high school? Had she refused his advances sending him into a fit of uncontrolled rage and beaten the girl to near death?

He told the police that after lunching with his father he went to a shoe store. A police officer was quickly sent to the store where an employee said that Robert Blackford had indeed been at the store and purchased a pair of shoes that day during the time Robert had said he was there.

Both Charles and Robert Blackford were eliminated from the list of possible suspects.

The police stated that a pencil was found on the floor next to the girl's body and the elder Blackford told them that Mina never went to the stockroom without a pencil to record merchandise taken from the shelves.

Young Blackford remembered that just before they had left for lunch his father asked Mina to type up an order and send it by telegram.

The police went to the Western Union office, just across the street from the Judd building where they interviewed Herbert Banning. The 17-year-old messenger who was sent to Behr-Manning.

Western Union records showed that the messenger left for Behr-Manning at 12:46 pm and returned to the office at 12:49. Herbert Banning was escorted across the street by the police officers to the scene of the grizzly attack.

Mina Dekker's ex-boyfriend John Schafer. Courtesy of Philip Morton, True Crime Library.

He told the police when he walked into the Behr-Manning office he saw Miss Dekker sitting at the typewriter. He did not talk to her nor did she talk to him. The order was sitting on the corner of the desk as it usually was. He told police that he picked it up and left the building.

The boy saw Mina Dekker at 12:48 and her brutally beaten body was discovered at 1:27 leaving the police with a 39-minute time frame in which the crime had occurred.

The next to be checked by the police was the story Ray Peters had told them of his whereabouts prior to discovering the bloody body of Mina Dekker.

His father-in-law, a county deputy, told the police he had driven Peters to the license bureau to buy plates for his car. But he could not verify what his son-in law had done afterwards.

The police went to the Kresge 5 & 10 where Peters said he had lunched on fried perch. No one remembered him being there, but they had a very busy lunch hour.

Peters could have been involved with the killing of Mina Dekker yet the police could think of no motive for Peters to cruelly murder the girl.

The evidence the police gathered led them to develop two theories as to the death of the young stenographer at the Behr-Manning Abrasive Company.

The first theory was that since the Judd Building was located in an area where indigent and transient people were known to gather, that a disreputable person slipped in the rear of the building, took the freight elevator up to the third floor and killed the young woman in the office. Possibly the degenerate person had been in the unoccupied second or fourth floors and knew when the pretty young woman was left alone.

They theorized that possibly when Mina Dekker heard a noise in the stockroom and she went to investigate and she was assaulted.

The delivery man Calvin De Blaey. Courtesy of Philip Morton, True Crime Library.

The Grand Rapids Herald

FIFTY-THIRD YEAR   GRAND RAPIDS, MICH., FRIDAY, MARCH 11, 1966   ★ ★ ★   PRICE THREE CENTS

Sunday Closing Act Passed; Faces Referendum

POLICE HOLD SUSPECT IN DEKKER SLAYING

Action Follows
Second Lie Test

Calvin DeBlaey Booked for Further
Inquiry; Shuns "Truth Serum"

Another theory the police developed was that the killer was a person who she might have known who wanted to purchase something from the stockroom. When she went to the stockroom, with her pencil in hand, she was struck from behind in the head with a hammer by the monstrous pathological murderer.

Miss Dekker's girlfriends told the police that the night before the tragic assault, Mina attended a friends wedding shower. At the shower Mina confided to a friend that she was afraid to go home alone at night. She told the friend that if she would walk with her she would tell something terrible.

The friend could not leave when Mina was ready so Mina walked with other girls to the bus stop where she paid the 10 cents for a six-block ride. This is something she would never have done, but rather than walk alone in the dark she felt safer on the bus.

What was it that had frightened Mina so much? What terrible thing was she going to confide with her friend?

The men engaged in a lunchtime game of cards on the first floor at the Manufacturers Supply Company during the murder were interviewed.

Each could speak for the other's whereabouts during the murder. Arthur Leopold and Roy Colby had been at the company's first floor storefront all through lunch.

Leopold told the police he thought he heard the rear door of the building slam shut about ten minutes before Mr. Peters came rushing in with the news of the bloodied woman he found, although, no one entered the Manufacturers Supply Company.

During the card game Colby said he thought he heard the freight elevator run but had thought nothing of it.

Colby and Leopold said that Calvin DeBlaey, the other man playing cards, had joined them just before Peters came in to report the ghastly sight he discovered.

DeBlaey was the twenty-seven year old delivery man for Manufacturers Supply Company. He told the police he was out making deliveries when the murder occurred and had only just returned.

When DeBlaey heard Leopold had told the police he had heard the rear door slam shut, DeBlaey told authorities that it was he who opened the door and let it slam shut.

Calvin DeBlaey said about 1:00 pm after making his last delivery, he drove back to the Judd Building and was entering the rear door when he decided he wanted a cup of coffee. He shut the door and walked to a nearby café, then at 1:15 pm joined the others in the card game.

When the police learned that Calvin DeBlaey had often gone to the third floor to visit with the pretty young stenographer working at the Behr-Manning Abrasives Company, they became very interested in Mr. DeBlaey.

Police Chief, Frank O'Malley requested Calvin take a lie detector test to clear his name. The delivery truck driver agreed and was driven by Chief O'-Malley to East Lansing to the Michigan State Police Crime Laboratory.

Chief O'Malley was notified the results of the test were inconclusive. It proved neither guilt nor innocence. The State Police sent the test results to Northwestern University, in Evanston, Illinois where experts in the field of lie detection would review them.

The experts at the university, after reviewing the information sent to them from East Lansing, suggested DeBlaey be tested again.

Calvin agreed to again submit to the test and the following day DeBlaey was driven to East Lansing by Chief O'Malley and Detectives Taylor and Breen where he underwent a second polygraph test.

When the test was completed, Calvin DeBlaey was asked to submit to being injected with scopolamine, also known as truth serum.

DeBlaey adamantly refused to allow any unknown substances to be injected into his body. The police tried for an hour to convince Calvin that it was in his best interest, that if he was telling the truth it would prove it, but he stood fast in his refusal.

Calvin was placed under arrest and held in the Grand Rapids jail. Two days later he agreed to undergo the injection of scopolamine. Afterward it was determined that Calvin DeBlaey was being truthful in his responses and released.

Calvin had passed the lie detector test yet he remained a person of interest in the vicious murder of Mina Dekker.

The Judd Building. Courtesy of Philip Morton, True Crime Library.

Weeks after the beating death and funeral of pretty Mina Dekker, Ray Peters, the shoe repairman who discovered her severely beaten body, approached Chief O'Malley of the Grand Rapids Police. He requested to be given a lie detector test.

Peters was never locked up for the crime, he was never even a suspect but he was being publicly vilified. Rumors were running rampant that it was he who had killed Mina Dekker. He wanted to take a lie detector test to prove his innocence in the death of the girl.

A test date was set but canceled. There is not a record of the test ever being taken by Peters.

Chief O'Malley told reporters that Peters was not a suspect in the vicious crime and called the treatment he was receiving shameful.

However shortly after the murder, a salesman, Mr. Norman, saw Peters' photograph in the newspaper and told the police that he had seen Peters at the Judd Building prior to the murder date.

Mr. Norman said he was going to the Behr-Manning Company on a sales visit when he saw Peters leaving the building. When he walked into the third floor office of Behr-Manning he found the stenographer, Mina Dekker, crying. He asked what was wrong and she responded that the man who just left had repaired a pair of shoes for her was giving her trouble.

The sales receipts of Peters shoe repair shop were searched and no record showed that Miss Dekker had work done by Peters. Mina's mother also told the police that Mina always used Monte's shoe repair and no one else.

Later in the month of the tragic murder of Mina Dekker the Detroit Police responded to the letter the Grand Rapids had sent out in mass to all police departments asking them to keep a look out for suspects.

An eighteen-year-old man in Detroit had been talking about the murder of a young woman in Grand Rapids and he just so happened to be in Grand Rapids on the day of the murder. Also of interest was the fact that he had scratches on the back of his hands.

After an intensive investigation, the young man had a sound alibi for the day and time of the Dekker killing.

THE ASTOUNDING PARSONS CASE NEW YORK'S CRIME CLASSIC

NOVEMBER 25¢

TRUE DETECTIVE

MYSTERIES AND FAMOUS DETECTIVE CASES

MURDER of the BEAUTIFUL TYPIST

Michigan's Baffling Mina Dekker Enigma ➔

HORROR at CAMP FUNSTON

THE GREAT WORLD SERIES BASEBALL MYSTERY BY ALAN HYND

COMPLETE BOOK LENGTH FEATURE

The sensational murder of the pretty young Grand Rapids woman was a feature story in True Detective Magazine.

The Grand Rapids police were called by a dry cleaner in the Grand Rapids area. Just days after the murder, a man had brought in a pair of trousers to be cleaned. The trousers were covered with dried blood from the knees down. Adding to the interest by the police was the fact that the man lived in the general area of the Judd Building.

Unfortunately the cleaner had cleaned the trousers before calling police. A chemist was called in to examine the trousers but he could not verify there was blood on the pants before the cleaning.

However an intriguing development, an in-depth investigation cleared the man of any involvement in the girl's murder.

.... How Could Anyone Be So Cruel As To Kill My Little Girl?

Weeks turned to months and months to years, tips were followed up on, people interviewed, but no arrests were made of the killer of Mina Dekker. Ray Peters lived a fretful life, ultimately committing suicide. In the letter he left to his family he did not say anything about Mina Dekker.

The Dekker file was passed from retiring detectives to detectives at the beginning of their careers and then on from them to the next generation. The person who so viciously assaulted the pretty young stenographer that a piece of her skull was thrown from her head and left her on the floor in a coagulating pool of her own blood has never been arrested, brought to trial, or served a day in prison.

The murder of Mina Dekker is still an open case.

As police investigated and the newspapers reported on the murder of Mina Dekker, the citizens of Grand Rapids were reminded of another gruesome murder of a young woman thirty-two years earlier.

On the evening of November 15, 1905, Josephine Oom, a 22 year-old stenographer, her sister and brother were riding in a carriage along the Old East Bridge Street road.

Suddenly someone lunged from the darkness, grabbed the horses bridle, bringing it to a stop. The person dressed in a long dark coat and cap pulled out a .32 caliber pistol and shot twice at the passengers in the buggy.

Jennie Oom, Josephine's sister, was struck in the hand by a bullet, their younger brother escaped injury, but Josephine was shot and killed.

A man who called Josephine three times that day was a suspect in the murder, was interrogated at length, but never charged.

No one was arrested in the murder of Josephine Oom. Her murder remains an open case.

Sabotage Of A Commercial Aircraft

· ·

A United Airlines Boeing 247 transcontinental airliner departed Newark, New Jersey, October 10, 1933, with a final destination of Oakland, California. There were several scheduled stops en route, the first in Cleveland, Ohio where the plane took on fuel and mail. The second stop was in Chicago, Illinois but the aircraft never made it that far, the United Airlines Boeing 247, flying a tail number of NC13304 exploded and crashed to the ground.

The Boeing 247 was one of the most modern aircraft of its time. It entered service in 1933 as the first airplane to have an all metal body and landing gear that retracted into the body of the aircraft. New safety features included an automatic pilot and two-way radio communication.

The new airplane was equipped with two Pratt & Whitney S1-H1-G Wasp 550 hp engines that could push the aircraft along at a cruising speed of 188 miles per hour and a maximum ceiling of 25,387 feet above sea level.

The Boeing Company built seventy-six of their 247 models in 1933. United Airlines was so impressed with the aircraft they purchased seventy of them.

With accommodations for ten passengers, the new 247 had improvement in passenger comfort. Soundproofing was installed in the cabin, a lavatory was built into the cabin, reading lights and adjustable air vents were installed for each passenger. The cabin had thermostatically controlled heating and cooling.

On the fateful day of October 10, 1933, four passengers were making the trip from Cleveland to Chicago; 25 year old Fred Schendorf of Chicago, 15 year old Dorothy Dwyer of Massachusetts, K. Smith of Chicago and Warren Burris of Columbus, Ohio.

At the controls of the Boeing 247 were pilot Harold Tarrant and co-pilot A. T. Ruby both from Oak Park, Illinois. Aboard the flight to accommodate the passenger's needs was the 26-year-old Stewardess, Alice Scribner from Chicago.

The flight from Cleveland was going well, they were on time and the pilot radioed in that all was well. Suddenly at 8:46 pm, while the plane was fifty miles out of Chicago, flying at an altitude of 1,000 feet, an explosion ripped through the Boeing 247.

Residents of Chesterton, Indiana heard the explosion and looked up in the night sky to see an airplane gyrating erratically towards the ground with flames shooting out of it. The flaming mass crashed in a wooded area and a second explosion rocked the silence of the night sending a ball of fire hundreds of feet into the air.

The tail section of the Boeing was ripped from the fuselage by the first explosion and crashed to earth nearly a mile from the main crash site.

All persons aboard the aircraft, passengers, pilots and stewardess were killed.

Federal investigators quickly responded to the crash site to search for a reason the airplane fell from the sky. The aircraft was not quite two months old, the pilots were experienced and competent and United Airlines had such a stringent safety policy that it was the first fatal accident for United in over 40 million miles.

Experts examined the engines and determined they were operating correctly at the time of the explosion. They also inspected the fuel tanks and found that they were intact and were not the cause for the initial explosion.

Further investigation by the United States Bureau of Investigation, under the direction of Melvin Purvis, head of he Chicago office, produced some perplexing evidence.

The baggage compartment and the cabin lavatory were more severely damaged than the rest of the aircraft. Those sections were blown into shreds while the rest of the airplane only displayed damage from the impact with the ground and resulting explosion.

Another interesting discovery was that the inside of the lavatory door had been punctured by hundreds of shards of metal while the cabin side of the door showed no such damage.

The evidence led the investigators to believe the Boeing 247 was brought down by an explosive device placed in the baggage compartment near the rear of the aircraft. The forensics further showed everything in front of the baggage compartment showed signs of being blown forward and everything behind the compartment was blown towards the rear.

Wreckage of the aircraft was taken to the Crime Detection Laboratory at Northwestern University in Evanston, Illinois. The experts there, in cooperation with the Porter County coroner's office, determined the crash of the Boeing 247 aircraft was the result of an explosive device, possibly containing nitroglycerin, being detonated while the airplane was in flight.

The practically new United Airlines Boeing 247, equipped with state of the art technology, had plummeted to the earth after a bomb exploded, ripping the tail assembly from the aircraft.

The downing of the Chicago bound United Airlines Boeing 247 was the first proven act of sabotage of a commercial airliner in the United States history of flight.

Another macabre first for the books was that Stewardess Alice Scribner, a licensed nurse in her first month on the job was the first United Airlines stewardess killed in a plane crash.

The United States Bureau of Investigation turned its attention from determining what was responsible for bringing the aircraft down to who was responsible for bringing it down.

The investigation was multi-directional. Reports came into their office that one of the passengers took a suspicious looking package wrapped in brown paper aboard the airplane. The mysterious package seemed like the likely source of the explosion but when the package was found in the wreckage still intact it was ruled out and the passenger who took it aboard was no more of a suspect than any other of the passengers aboard the doomed flight.

They investigated a rifle that was found in the wreckage, but it was owned by a passenger who was flying to Chicago to compete in a competition at the Chicago North Shore Gun Club.

Baggage handlers at Newark, New Jersey and Cleveland, Ohio were interviewed but no one with access to the baggage compartment proved to be a person of interest. There was no reason for the passengers or crew to detonate an explosive on the airplane killing themselves and the others. All leads the Bureau investigated went nowhere.

To this day there has not been anyone charged or convicted of the October 10, 1933 bombing of the United Airlines Boeing 247 over Chesterton, Indiana; the first proven act of sabotage in commercial aviation.

Who Murdered Pixie?

The pretty, 5 foot 8 inch blonde lifeguard was a favorite of the youngsters who swam in the pool. She was also a favorite of some of the adults and staff who frequented the pool.

Mary Beth Grismore, nicknamed "Pixie," was a beauty queen from Iowa, a Miss Iowa runner-up. She married Robert Hale and moved from Iowa to his home in rural Parke County near Marshall, Indiana. During the ten years of their marriage they became the proud parents of two sons.

As sometimes happens, Robert and Pixie grew apart and were divorced. While working at the Turkey Run State Park as a lifeguard and gate attendant, Pixie met Patrick Ralston.

Ralston was quite taken with the brown-eyed beauty that worked at the same park he did. He soon began spending more time around the pool area.

In July of 1977, the two began a romantic relationship, spending as much time as they could in each other's company. At least as much time as a married man and father of two could.

Ralston's wife required surgery after the birth of their second child and needed to recuperate at her parent's house in Terre Haute, Indiana. With his wife away for a while, his affair with the ex-beauty queen took on a new intensity and in just months Ralston filed for a divorce from his wife.

In January, Pat Ralston was injured in a workplace accident requiring a week's stay in the hospital and a lengthy period of recovery. During this time, the affair between Pat and Pixie cooled and Pat rekindled the relationship with his wife.

Also, in a move that shocked Pixie's friends in Indiana, just after Christmas she married a farmer from Corydon, Iowa, and was going to move back to her home state and live a short distance from her childhood home.

Pat, the married man and Pixie, the divorcee, had gone their separate ways and each found love outside their affair, he with his wife and she with a man back home.

But the allure of meeting one last time for old times sake got the better of them both and they planned to meet at the Holiday Inn in Cloverland, Indiana... room 215.

Pixie had left a decade of her life in the rural home outside of Marshall, Indiana. In early 1978, she drove her new husband's 1973 silver metallic blue Thunderbird with a dark blue vinyl top to Indiana to pack up her belongings and say farewell to her Indiana friends.

Mary Beth "Pixie" Grismore

On the evening of February 21, 1978, Pixie and two good friends drove to Terre Haute for a going away bash. They went to dinner, took in a movie and went club hopping for drinks and dancing.

The three women returned to Marshall about 1:30 AM. Before departing, the women made plans to meet the following day to help Pixie pack up the decades worth of belongings.

The next morning the two women met at Pixie's house to help pack but Pixie and the Thunderbird were not there.

Thinking she had gone out for breakfast or as anyone who has ever moved knows, in search of more boxes, they waited, but Pixie never came back.

The boxes packed with the kid's toys, the clothes, even Pixie's purse were there, but Pixie never showed up.

After a fretful few days, the family of Pixie Grismore notified the Parke County Sheriff's Department that their daughter was missing.

On February 22, 1978, the day she was to return to Corydon, Iowa, the pretty blonde, brown-eyed Miss Iowa runner-up vanished.

Parke County Sheriff's Department started a missing person investigation. They interviewed Pixie's ex-husband and her current husband. Neither man was considered a suspect in her disappearance.

The days when nothing was heard from Pixie turned into weeks and her whereabouts were not known.

Pixie's parents traveled from Iowa and spent weeks talking with residents of Marshall seeking any information they could about their missing daughter.

Who Murdered Pixie?

The parents established a reward in hopes of enticing someone who knew something about the disappearance of their daughter to come forward. They also hired a psychic, Greta Alexander, hoping she could shed some light on the location of their beautiful daughter.

The psychic proclaimed that a man was lying in wait at Pixie's house, waiting for her to return from the night out on the town with her girlfriends. When Pixie returned, the man shot the pretty blonde in the head. The Psychic told the parents that the body of Pixie Grismore was dumped on the grounds of the Turkey Run State Park and her silver metallic blue Thunderbird would be found in another location.

A Parke County deputy drove Miss Alexander through the park hoping she would recognize something that would trigger her psychic powers and she would lead them to the body, but she wasn't able to add any other information.

The investigation revealed that prior to her disappearance, Pixie had told a friend that she had received several prank calls. The phone would ring at her rural Parke County home, but when she answered the caller would not say anything.

On May 3, 1978, the Whitehall, Ohio police were called to the Whitehall Holiday Inn. The desk clerk told the police that a car had been left in their parking lot and it had been there for an extended period of time.

A car left in the motel parking lot hadn't created suspicion because the motel was near the Columbus, Ohio airport and travelers often left their vehicles in the lot while they were away on a trip.

Motel employees became suspicious of the car when it had been there for almost two months and they noticed the license plate had been removed.

The police looked through the windows into the interior of the 1973 silver metallic blue Thunderbird with a dark blue vinyl top but did not see anything suspicious.

But when they pried open the trunk of the Thunderbird, the police were met with the horrible stench of rotting flesh from the decayed human body within.

The authorities suspected the body found in the car trunk was that of Mary Beth Grismore. She was missing and the body was found in the trunk of a car answering the description of Mary Beth's vehicle, but due to the advanced state of decomposition of the body, identification could not be visibly made. The body was so decayed it was impossible to tell if the victim was male or female.

All that was known for sure was that the victim lying in the trunk of the Thunderbird had been murdered, the police could tell by the rope wrapped tightly around its neck.

To make a positive identification of the body, the Parke County coroner requested the dental records of 26-year-old Mary Beth Grismore.

The dental records proved the identity of the decaying corpse found in the Thunderbird to be that of the pretty, ex-beauty queen Pixie Grismore.

The police theorized that the murder of the young woman had occurred at the house near Marshall, Indiana and her body was transported across state lines to the motel in Ohio where it was found.

Since the killer or killers crossed state lines in the commission of a crime, the case became the jurisdiction of the Federal Bureau of Investigation.

The Thunderbird was taken to the Ohio State Police crime lab and searched for clues that might lead authorities to the identity of the killer, while a forensic autopsy was preformed on the body of Pixie Grismore.

The only clue that the FBI had to work on was the rope found around Mrs. Grismore's throat.

In the course of their investigation, the FBI interviewed Patrick Ralston. He told them that he knew Pixie since they both worked at Turkey Run State Park, but the relationship had not gone beyond a friendly work related point.

The FBI suspected there was more to Ralston's story and brought him in for a second interview.

Under intense interrogation, Ralston finally admitted that he and Pixie were more than casual coworkers, that he had a romantic relationship with the beautiful lifeguard.

With his dishonesty in the first interview, Patrick Ralston shot to the top of the list of suspects.

The FBI suspected that Patrick Ralston had murdered Pixie Grismore but they did not have any solid evidence on which to build a case.

The case of the murder of the pretty lifeguard, the Miss Iowa runner-up, had gone cold.

No other evidence, no other suspects surfaced. For years the FBI waited for a new clue to come to light or for a guilt riddled person to confess, but no one came forward.

In 1998, almost twenty years after the disappearance and ultimate death of Pixie Grismore, information was released about the case in the November issue of *The Dispatcher Magazine*.

The magazine reported that when questioning Patrick Ralston in 1978, he told the FBI a startling story, a story that had not been made public for twenty years.

Ralston told the FBI that when he and Pixie had met for their farewell rendezvous at the Cloverdale, Indiana Holiday Inn, Pixie told him she had done something she had always wanted to do.

In the late 1970s she was a county coordinator for the re-election campaign of long time United States Senator Birch Bayh of Indiana, and before she moved back to Iowa she made arrangements through the senator's chief of staff to have drinks with the senator.

Ralston related that Pixie had told him that she partied with the senator and his entourage in an Indianapolis motel bar then went with the senator to his room. She told Ralston that she had sex with the senator and stayed the night with him.

The FBI verified the Senator was a registered guest at the Indianapolis motel on the day Pixie told Ralston she met with the senator. But, the authorities could neither prove nor disprove Pixie's story. It was another path the investigation took that went nowhere.

Over three decades after the murder of Mary Beth "Pixie" Grismore, her murder remains unsolved. Could Pixie have been killed by a person known to her but not yet known by the authorities, was it an act of a jealous ex-boyfriend, possibly a political cover up, or was it just a random killing by a person unknown to Pixie? The truth might never be discovered, or possibly new evidence might come to light that would lead to the conviction of the murderer.

The public information officer for the Indiana State Police reports the Grismore case is still an open investigation. Anyone with information or tips regarding the case should telephone the agency's hotline at 1-800-453-4756.

Gone And Never Seen Again

Josephine stared out of the window of her house, watching the reflective orange glow of the setting sun shimmering off the rippled surface of Square Lake. She looked at the lake but didn't see it, her mind was preoccupied; it had been hours since he called saying he would be right home. He had not arrived.

Josephine's husband, Jimmy Riddle Hoffa, the 62-year-old labor leader once said: "If you get knocked down and kicked, you get up and kick back harder." This quote best described Mr. Hoffa's attitude in life. Far from a simple beginning, he rose to be the General President of the United States' largest labor union.

Born in Brazil, Indiana, Jimmy's coal miner father died when he was just a boy and Jimmy and his mother moved to Detroit.

Jimmy began his career in the organized labor movement in the 1930s when he was just a teenager working at a Kroger Grocery Company warehouse, unloading railroad cars in southwest Detroit. Young Hoffa, upset over the low pay, long hours, and poor working conditions, organized a strike on the day the

Former International Brotherhood of the Teamsters General President, James R. Hoffa.

company was receiving a large shipment of fresh fruit. The company, faced with spoilage of the perishable cargo and a huge financial loss, settled with the workers.

From this beginning, Jimmy Hoffa became a labor organizer and eventually president of Local 299 in Detroit.

The five-foot-five-inch Hoffa became known as a hard nose organizer with the International Brotherhood of Teamsters in Detroit. Hoffa took over the leadership of a failing local union with few members and even less funding. Through cunning, and some say fear and intimidation, Hoffa grew the union to over 5,000 members with a substantial bank account.

Hoffa and the Teamster's efforts to organize workers into unions was not readily accepted by owners and management. During his 1932 – 1975 tenure as a union organizer, Hoffa's car was blown apart by a bomb, his office was broken into and destroyed, he received many threats and beatings and he was arrested dozens of times.

In addition to management, which opposed Hoffa's organizing efforts, other unions competed to represent a company's workers, sometimes violently.

Hoffa, through his tenacity, succeeded and in 1952 became a national Vice President of the International Brotherhood of Teamsters. Six years later Jimmy Hoffa became the national General President of the union, an office he would hold until 1971.

During this time, the International Brotherhood of Teamsters became the largest labor union in the nation with over one and a half million members. In 1964, the Teamsters, largely under Hoffa's guidance, negotiated the first nationwide contract for over-the-road truck drivers.

Beginning in 1957, Jimmy Hoffa faced a decade of governmental scrutiny. After a lengthy investigation, Hoffa was charged with receiving a one million dollar kickback in return for his guarantee that a company would not suffer any labor issues.

After years of pretrial haggling, the case went to trial. The jury found Hoffa innocent of the charges, but shortly after being found not guilty, Hoffa was arrested, tried and found guilty of jury tampering for bribing at least two of the jurors in the case.

In just months, Hoffa was convicted for both jury tampering and mail fraud. For both convictions he was sentenced to a total of thirteen years in a federal penitentiary.

For three years, Hoffa attorneys appealed the convictions before all appeals were exhausted and Hoffa began serving his sentence in 1967 at the Lewisburg Federal Penitentiary in Pennsylvania.

A group photo of a 1950 hunting trip at the Hoffa camp near Iron Mountain, Michigan. Jimmy Hoffa is the fifth from the left and David Johnson is second from right. From the personal collection of David Johnson Jr.

Before entering prison, Hoffa hand selected his successor as General President of the International Brotherhood of Teamsters, Frank Fitzsimmons.

Frank Fitzsimmons was a long-term friend of Hoffa's and shared a similar background. He began his labor union career in Detroit as a truck driver in 1935. He joined Local 299 and he and the president, Jimmy Hoffa, became close friends.

Fitzsimmons followed his friend into Teamster politics and was made the Local 299 business manager in 1936. In 1940 he was elected Local 299 vice president, and in 1961 Fitzsimmons was elected an international union vice president. He was Hoffa's right hand man who stuck with him through all of Hoffa's highs and lows.

Hoffa chose Fitzsimmons as the General President of the International Brotherhood of Teamsters with the agreement that when Hoffa was released from prison, Hoffa would regain his position.

However, once Hoffa began serving his sentence, Fitzsimmons took steps to distance himself from Hoffa. Hoffa had developed the Teamsters in a top down hierarchy to provide himself with unquestioned control.

Fitzsimmons changed the organizational structure of the National Teamsters to be more decentralized, a move that infuriated Hoffa. Fitzsimmons also infuriated Hoffa by firing Hoffa's wife, Josephine from her well paying position as head of the Teamsters Women's "DRIVE" committee and he also fired Hoffa's son, James P. Hoffa, from his job as an attorney for the union.

After serving nearly five years of his thirteen-year sentence, President Nixon commuted Jimmy Hoffa's sentence in 1971 to time served. However, as part of the commutation agreement Hoffa could not partake in any union activity until 1980.

Just a year later, the International Brotherhood of Teamsters endorsed Richard Nixon, a Republican, in his re-election campaign. Even though the union had in elections past always supported the democratic candidate.

Freed from prison but not able to regain his position as General President of the International Brotherhood of the Teamsters, Hoffa appealed to the U.S. Court of Appeals to overturn his forced hiatus from the union. He argued that the government was depriving him of his right to pursue a career of his choice and that he wasn't aware of the clause at the time he accepted the agreement.

Fitzsimmons supported the government's position that Hoffa be banished from direct or indirect union involvement. It was the government's stance, although, many believe it was the union itself that requested the clause preventing Hoffa's involvement in union activities.

Jimmy Hoffa was publicly critical of Fitzsimmons' leadership of the Teamsters and was making plans to regain his leadership role once the commutation agreement was altered to allow him to resume union involvement.

International Brotherhood of Teamsters General President Frank Fitzsimmons and President Richard Nixon. This photograph is in the public domain.

Hoffa threatened to write a book about the Teamsters under the leadership of Fitzsimmons. The book would reveal, Hoffa said, how Fitzsimmons had sold out the union to mobsters and had made large, low or no interest loans from the Teamsters pension fund to "Mob" related businesses. That the Teamsters had a strong relationship with the Mafia, a relationship that had long been under scrutiny by the government.

The two men, Jimmy Hoffa and Frank Fitzsimmons, who stood side by side fighting management goons, who were arrested for their union organizing activities, who rose within the Teamsters to the highest of positions, and who were once the closest of friends, were now bitter enemies.

Knowing that he had lost influence on the national union level, Hoffa set his sights on regaining the leadership of Local 299, the Detroit union where the Hoffa name still had clout. From there he planned to challenge Fitzsimmons for the office of national general president.

During this time, Local 299 was locked in a period of mayhem. Union officials had been the victim of bombings, beatings and shootings. The violence was drawing the attention of the national union and the federal authorities as well. Publicly the national and local Teamsters called for the violence to cease and blamed it on radicals outside the union, but most people connected with Local 299 knew the hostility was the result of the struggle between members who were allies of Jimmy Hoffa and those who supported Frank Fitzsimmons.

The president of Local 299, 68-year-old David Johnson, a Hoffa ally, was severely beaten by another Teamster Union member in 1970.

The hostility continued in 1971 when homes of two Teamsters business agents were bombed. Also a barn on a farm owned by the Local 299 Secretary-Treasurer was burned to the ground.

David Johnson was again a victim of violence in 1972 when two windows in his office were shattered by shotgun blasts. The same year George Roxburgh, a Local 299 Trustee, was sitting in his car in Royal Oak, Michigan when a shotgun blast shattered his car window striking him in the face. He was severely injured but lived.

In 1974, the 45-foot cabin cruiser docked on a canal behind the house of David Johnson on Grosse Ile, an island in the Detroit River, exploded.

David and his wife Anne were in Port Charlotte, FL. preparing their retirement home at the time of the explosion. It was first thought an auxiliary fuel tank on the boat had accidentally exploded, but divers found the auxiliary tank intact and evidence that the explosion was intentionally set. Johnson

David Johnson, President of Local 299 and ally of Jimmy Hoffa. From the collection of David Johnson Jr.

openly said Teamster politics were responsible for sending his beloved boat, "Big Mac" to the bottom of a Grosse Ile canal.

David Johnson had intended to retire from his position as president of the 18,000 member Local 299, but after his boat was destroyed, he openly vowed to run for re-election and when the provision that prevented Hoffa from any union involvement was reversed, he would appoint Hoffa as his administrative assistant. Johnson also publicly supported Hoffa for the presidency of Local 299 to use it as a springboard to help Hoffa challenge Fitzsimmons for the National presidency.

If Johnson sought reelection, he would be running against Local 299 vice president Richard Fitzsimmons, son of the International Brotherhood of Teamsters General President Frank Fitzsimmons and staunch enemy of Jimmy Hoffa.

More violence rocked Local 299 when the Lincoln Continental owned by Local 299 and provided to the union's Vice President, Richard Fitzsimmons, mysteriously exploded just blocks from Detroit's Tiger Stadium, an act that was generally agreed to be retribution for the destruction of Johnson's boat.

Authorities convened a special investigation unit to probe the violence. Most Local 299 officials were called to testify, as was Jimmy

Hoffa, however Hoffa was a belligerent and reluctant witness, refusing to answer questions.

National Teamsters General President, Frank E. Fitzsimmons termed the violence that was rocking Local 299 in Detroit "insane."

Hoffa said when he was released from prison; "Tell the rats to get off the ship because I'm coming back." Hoffa openly claimed when he regained the leadership of the Teamsters he would clean house.

Although he was often reputed to be a close friend of the Mafia throughout his union career, Hoffa detested the influence the "mob" had under Fitzsimmons regime. Low interest or no interest loans were made from the multi-million dollar Teamsters pension fund to mob related businesses, many in Las Vegas.

The leaders of the mob did not want to lose access to the millions of dollars from the pension fund and Jimmy Hoffa posed a threat to its future development of its lucrative Las Vegas properties.

On the morning of July 30, 1975, Jimmy Hoffa received a call at his Square Lake summer home, some 20 miles north of Detroit; the call apparently confirmed a meeting between Hoffa and an unknown person. He told his wife one person he was going to meet was his long time friend, Anthony Giacalone.

David Johnson on his 45-foot cabin cruiser, "Big Mac" before it was destroyed by an explosion. From the collection of David Johnson Jr.

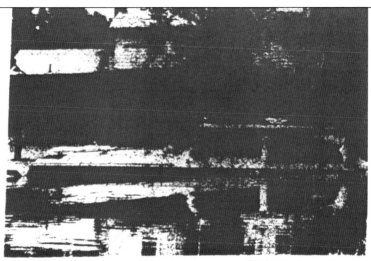

Johnson's boat rests on bottom of a Grosse Ile canal

Rivals in Union Sank Boat, Teamster Leader Charges

Anthony Giacalone, aka, "Tony Jack" was a well-known, high-ranking figure in the Detroit mafia.

On July 30, 1975 at 1:15, Hoffa kissed his wife goodbye and drove his green Pontiac Grand Ville to Airport Service Lines, a limousine service that served Detroit's Metropolitan Airport and operated out of Pontiac Airport.

The Airport Service Lines is owned and operated by Louis "The Pope" Linteau who was the former president of Teamsters Local 614. At one time Linteau and Hoffa did not get along, in fact it was said they were enemies. But recently the two had become close friends.

Linteau acted as a go between for persons wishing to meet with Hoffa. Investigators believe the people Hoffa was going to meet had arranged the meeting though Louis Linteau.

Hoffa stopped at the Airport Service Lines office on the way to the Machus Red Fox restaurant to talk with Linteau, he wanted Linteau to attend the meeting with him but Linteau was not in.

An employee at the Airport Service Line office later recalled that he had overheard Jimmy Hoffa say he was going to the Machus Red Fox restaurant to meet with "Tony G."

It is theorized that Hoffa's July 30, 1975 meeting with Tony Jack had been arranged through Linteau.

Hoffa left the airport en route to the Machus Red Fox restaurant, on the corner of Telegraph and Maple roads in Bloomfield Township where he was to meet with Tony Jack and possibly others.

The manager of the upscale restaurant said later that Hoffa never entered the restaurant. They would remember, the restaurant requires coat and tie and Hoffa was dressed in a blue pull over shirt.

Witnesses that had seen Hoffa reported he parked in the north end of the parking lot apparently waiting for someone to arrive.

At 2:30 Hoffa went to a strip mall behind the restaurant and telephoned his wife. He asked if Giacalone had called the home to change the plans because no one had arrived.

He also called Louis Linteau to see if the plans had changed. Hoffa then went back to the restaurant parking lot to wait.

A real estate salesman saw Hoffa in his car in the parking lot and spoke with him briefly. The time was approximately 2:45.

He was one of the last people to see the former Teamsters General President... for Jimmy Hoffa disappeared on that July day in 1975.

Josephine called her children deeply concerned about the well being of their father. Their son James P. Hoffa was vacationing in Traverse City and their daughter Barbara Hoffa Crancer, a judge, who lived in suburban St. Louis, Missouri shared their mother's concern and began to make arrangements to travel to the Hoffa home.

Throughout the night, no word came from Hoffa nor were his whereabouts discovered.

The next day the Hoffa family asked the Pontiac Police to check the Machus Red Fox restaurant parking lot for the green Pontiac Grand Ville with a green vinyl top belonging to Jimmy Hoffa. The request was referred to the Bloomfield Township Police.

Jimmy Hoffa's unlocked car was found in the lot. A quick search of the interior of the car revealed nothing to indicate a struggle or that Hoffa had been abducted, killed or simply walked away from the vehicle.

Hoffa's car was towed to the police impound lot for a more thorough search.

The keys were not in the ignition so police could not open the trunk. Once James P. Hoffa, Jimmy's son, gave permission, firemen pried the trunk open. Possibly expecting to find the body of Jimmy Hoffa inside, the police found nothing of importance in the trunk.

Great Lakes Cold Case Files...

At 6:00 PM of July 31, the Hoffa family filed a missing person report with the Detroit Police Department. Jimmy Hoffa became Missing Person #75-3425.

Hours turned to days and Jimmy Hoffa had not contacted his wife or family. The family said Jimmy was a creature of habit and he always told friends or family where he was going and with whom he was meeting. Yet Hoffa had not contacted anyone since he last called Linteau and his wife to question if Anthony Giacalone had called to change the meeting.

The Bloomfield Township Police and the Michigan State Police conferred and continued to search for evidence in the disappearance of Jimmy Hoffa. The Hoffa car was searched, employees of the Machus Red Fox restaurant were questioned, and witnesses who came forward were interviewed. The police surveyed a five-mile radius of the restaurant by helicopter looking in drainage ditches, wooded lots and the five lakes within the area.

The Federal Bureau of Investigation joined the local police and the Michigan State Police in the investigation five days following Hoffa's disappearance.

The Detroit office of the F.B.I. assigned almost 275 agents to the Hoffa case and the Director promised more if needed.

The authorities, after an extensive investigation, developed a short list of who they suspected were responsible for the Hoffa disappearance.

The authorities and newspaper investigative reporters independently adopted the same theory; Jimmy Hoffa had become too much of an annoyance to organized crime and they needed to remove the problem to retain their control of the Teamster's pension fund.

Despite thousands of hours spent by authorities, hundreds of tips from citizens, years of investigation and hundreds of typed pages of interviews, no one has ever been arrested in connection with the disappearance of Jimmy Hoffa.

After a multi-year investigation, the Federal Bureau of Investigation published their finding of the disappearance of Jimmy Hoffa. In the 50+ page "Hoffex Memo" of 1976, but not made public until 1985, various theories of why Jimmy Hoffa was abducted and several people who are suspects involved in Hoffa's disappearance were listed.

The motive for Hoffa's disappearance most often talked about involves Hoffa's desire to return to Teamster Union politics.

Hoffa told friends and family that he expected the provision of his pardon prohibiting him for any direct or indirect union involvement to be lifted soon. That would have opened the door for Hoffa to seek the union's national presidency.

General President James Hoffa proceeding over a International Brotherhood of Teamsters convention.

F.B.I. sources say that some people did not want Hoffa to regain the power of the national office because he would not be as easy to manipulate as Frank Fitzsimmons was.

Another motive for the decision to remove Hoffa was because Hoffa was threatening to talk to a government agency, probably the Justice Department, about union activities. He possibly was going to make public the Teamsters participation in kickbacks and other illegal activities that violated labor relation laws.

There were many in the union who did not want the government becoming involved in their business. Possibly Hoffa was shut up to avoid a government investigation of the nation's largest labor union.

One more motive for the disappearance and possible murder of Hoffa presented by the F.B.I. in the Hoffex Memo is the volatile relationship between Jimmy Hoffa and Anthony "Tony Pro" Provenzano.

The two men were bitter enemies and it is said that the topic of the meeting Jimmy Hoffa was going to attend on July 30, 1975 was to patch up the differences of the two. It is also reported that Tony Pro was going to be at the meeting.

Hoffa had declined several requests for meeting with Tony Pro in the past and why he would accept a meeting on the date of his disappearance is unknown.

In the Hoffex Memo the F.B.I. lists persons of interest. They were; Anthony "Tony Jack" Giacalone, Anthony "Tony Pro" Provenzano, Chuckie O'Brien, Thomas and Stephen Andretta, Salvatore "Sally Bugs" Briguglio and Gabriel Briguglio.

Weather
Cooler
Details on Page III

The Detroit News

AMERICA'S LARGEST EVENING CIRCULATION

182nd YEAR NO. 348

TUESDAY, AUGUST 5, 1975

15 CENTS

"It's very likely we'll never find his body. This is the type of case we never find a solution to."

FBI convinced Hoffa is dead, source says

Anthony "Tony Jack" Giacalone was a longtime friend of Hoffa's. Tony Jack was known to be a Detroit Mafia capo with a long history of involvement with organized crime. He began as a bookmakers' runner and later became an enforcer and rose in the organization under Detroit crime boss Joseph Zerilli. His career was rather low key, avoiding publicity until the Hoffa disappearance. The F.B.I. in their "Hoffex Memo" say Tony Jack was one of the men it was believed Hoffa was meeting on July 30, 1975.

F.B.I. files indicate Anthony Provenzano, "Tony Pro," a captain in the Genovese crime family of New York City also held the position of vice president in the International Brotherhood of Teamsters Local 560 in Union City, New Jersey. The F.B.I. reported that Hoffa was going to meet with both Anthony Giacalone and Anthony Provenzano on the day he disappeared.

Jimmy Hoffa and Tony Pro were once close friends. Tony Pro was credited with delivering the backing of the Eastern Teamsters when Hoffa first ran for national president of the union. Hoffa in turn awarded Tony Pro by helping him climb the ladder to the vice president of International Brotherhood of Teamsters.

Both Provenzano and Hoffa were sentenced to serve time in Lewisburg Federal Prison where Tony Pro's connections in the crime world made him well respected among the prisoners, and he welcomed Hoffa under his umbrella of protection.

Weather
Hot
Details on Page 2A

The Detroit News

Races
Page 5B

182nd YEAR NO. 345

SATURDAY MORNING, AUGUST 2, 1975

15 CENTS

Reward largest in 'Secret Witness' history

$25,000 is offered in Hoffa case

Tony Pro received a pardon from President Nixon with the provision that he could not have direct or indirect involvement in union activities for five years as part of his parole. However, it was well known that despite the sanction, he called the shots in Local 560.

The two friends had a falling-out it is said because Hoffa was unable or unwilling to secure a union backed loan for Tony Pro for a restaurant he wanted to open. The rift between the two grew to the point they became bitter enemies. Once they met by chance and had a violent confrontation, supposedly involving a fistfight and broken bottles.

Hoffa publicly opposed Tony Pro's desire to officially return to his role in Local 560 and Tony Pro strongly resisted Hoffa in his attempt to regain the presidency of the national union.

Another F.B.I. person of interest was the un-official son of Jimmy Hoffa, Charles "Chuckie" O'Brien.

O'Brien was often called the "Adopted" son of Jimmy Hoffa. "Chuckie" O'Brien moved to Detroit in the 1930's when his mother, Sylvia, got a job with the Teamsters.

Sylvia O'Brien met and became a close friend of Josephine Hoffa, Jimmy's wife and when Sylvia married, Chuckie moved in with the Hoffa family. Jimmy raised Chuckie as one of his own.

In 1964, Hoffa signed papers to formalize the adoption however, they were never filed in court. At eighteen years of age, O'Brien became a business agent with Local 299 where Jimmy was then president.

Chuckie was close to Hoffa yet he was also close to Anthony Giacalone. Chuckie's mother, Sylvia, was a friend with Tony Jack for many years. They were so close that Chuckie referred to Tony Jack as 'Uncle Tony.'

Thomas and Stephen Andretta were brothers who were reputed to be in Anthony Provenzano's inner circle of the union. The F.B.I. alleges the brothers were bodyguards hired by Local 560 who were the muscle for enforcing union activities. They were suspected to be involved in killings which had union and mob connections, including the possible murder of Jimmy Hoffa.

The names of brothers Salvatore "Sally Bugs" and Gabriel "Gabe" Briguglio, two New Jersey Teamster Union members and associates of Tony Pro, are alleged to have mob ties and involvement with mob connected killings and are allegedly principle figures in the murder of Jimmy Hoffa.

Possible Abduction Scenario

The authorities have put together a theory of how the former International Teamsters Union President was abducted and killed. Their theory is based on evidence from the days, weeks, months and years following the July 30, 1975 disappearance of Jimmy Hoffa.

Jimmy Hoffa was a cautious man, he always had been. He hardly went anywhere or met with anyone without telling family or a business associate where, and with whom he was meeting. Thus for Jimmy to not call and follow up with a call to tell Josephine where he was going was highly unusual.

Being a cautious man, the authorities believe Hoffa would never have left his car at the Machus Red Fox unattended and unlocked, nor would he have willingly gotten into a car with anyone but persons he knew and with whom he was comfortable, leading them to believe Hoffa knew the abductors and possibly they were friends of his.

A man making a delivery to the Machus Red Fox and parked in the parking lot of the restaurant came forward and provided investigators a major lead.

He told police, he observed Jimmy Hoffa in the back right-hand seat of a maroon, 1975 Mercury Marquis Brougham. He also identified Chuckie O'Brien in the vehicle along with two other men he did not know. He said he thought he saw something under a blanket between Hoffa and another man in the back of the car that looked like a rifle or shotgun.

The police gave the delivery man a polygraph test that indicated he was being truthful in his deposition.

Based on the description of the vehicle, the police determined a car matching that description was owned by Joey Giacalone, son of Anthony

"Tony Jack" Giacalone, one of the men it was said Hoffa was to meet that day.

The police impounded the car and made a thorough search of it, looking for clues that could tie the vehicle to Hoffa's disappearance.

Specially trained police dogs were flown into Detroit from Philadelphia to aid in the investigation. The dogs were exposed to a pair of shorts and shoes known to have been recently worn by Hoffa.

Once they had Hoffa's scent, the dogs sniffed Joey Giacalone's maroon Mercury.

Both dogs had hits on the back seat of the mercury, indicating Hoffa had been in the back seat of the car recently. One of the dogs also indicated a scent in the trunk of the car. However it cannot be conclusively stated that Jimmy Hoffa was ever in the trunk of the Mercury based on the findings of the dog. The dog might have been sensing Hoffa's scent from the backseat through the seat material.

Joey Giacalone was interviewed by the authorities as to his involvement or the involvement of his Mercury in the disappearance of Jimmy Hoffa.

Giacalone had a sound alibi for the July 30, 1975 date. When asked about his car, he said he had loaned the car to a friend that day. The friend's name was Chuckie O'Brien, Jimmy Hoffa's trusted adopted son.

Chuckie O'Brien is a person the ever-cautious Jimmy Hoffa would not hesitate to get in a car with.

O'Brien admitted to using the car that day and fingerprints belonging to him were found in the car.

Another witness to seeing Hoffa in the rear seat of a car in the Machus Red Fox parking lot came forward saying she saw Jimmy Hoffa in a brown or maroon car in the parking lot of the restaurant.

Both of the witnesses, the delivery man and the woman, observed three "line-ups" in December of 1975 each containing one of three suspects; Thomas Andretta, Salvatore Briguglio and Gabriel Briguglio.

The delivery man could not identify any of the men as being in the Mercury with Hoffa but the woman did identify one of the suspects as a man she saw in the car with Hoffa on July 30, 1975 in the parking lot of the Machus Red Fox restaurant… Salvatore Briguglio.

Decades after Jimmy Hoffa disappeared, a DNA test was done on a hair found on the rear seat of Joey Giacalone's Mercury. The hair found in the car was an exact match for hair taken from Jimmy Hoffa's hairbrush, further indicating Hoffa's presence in the car.

It's thought that it was arranged through Louis Linteau that Hoffa would meet at the Machus Red Fox restaurant with Anthony "Tony Jack" Giacalone and Anthony "Tony Pro" Provenzano in an effort for Hoffa and "Tony Pro" to try to work out their differences.

However, the real reason for the meeting was not to make amends and discuss Hoffa's rise to the top of the union once again, but rather to remove Hoffa permanently from any future union involvement

Further, it s suspected that Chuckie O'Brien, knowing full well of the plans to kill Hoffa, lured Hoffa into the car he borrowed from Anthony Giacalone's son.

As part of the investigation, the F.B.I. followed up on the alibi's given by the men Hoffa was supposed to meet on the day of his disappearance.

Anthony "Tony Jack" Giacalone was at the Southfield Athletic Club most of the day. There were several people who witnessed his presence.

Anthony "Tony Pro" Provenzano had people who could verify he was in New Jersey on July 30, 1975.

Both men said they did not have an appointment to meet with Jimmy Hoffa that day.

So, where is Jimmy Hoffa?

The F.B.I. makes a strong case as to why Jimmy Hoffa was killed. It also makes a fairly strong case as to who killed him, but what is still open to conjecture is what happened to Jimmy Hoffa's body.

Decades after the disappearance of Hoffa on July 30, 1975, the mystery of what happened to him creates almost as much interest as the question; "Who shot JFK?"

It also seems that every year or so another theory as to where the remains of Hoffa lies surfaces.

Within days of the disappearance of the ex-National General President of the Teamsters, Local 299 announced they had offered a $25,000 reward. The offer of a cash reward brought in a deluge of tips.

The phones rang constantly at the Bloomfield Township police station and at the *Detroit News* newspaper office as a result of their "Secret Witness" program. Some were obvious jokesters, some were deranged individuals calling to take credit for killing Hoffa. Yet other tips had enough credence for the police to check them out.

One caller said that Jimmy Hoffa was seen outside a restaurant in Oakland County, Michigan and another man called to report that he had buried Hoffa in his basement.

Gone And Never Seen Again

A man from the small southwest Michigan town of Somerset called the tip line to report he was with Jimmy Hoffa when Hoffa was shot with a 12 gauge shotgun at close range and buried in a field. After an extensive search of the field, no evidence of the murder and subsequent burial was found.

Ironically, another credible tip came into the Secret Witness program switchboard from Somerset, Michigan. A woman claimed she had seen a body floating in a small lake in the area. An investigation by authorities turned up negative.

A woman who lived near a construction project at 12 Mile and Evergreen roads in the northern Detroit suburb of Southfield, called the Bloomfield Township police with an interesting occurrence.

She reported on August 1, 1975, just one day after Hoffa disappeared from the Machus Red Fox restaurant, that she and her husband were awakened at 2:30 in the morning by the sound of a speeding car followed by the sound of a bulldozer at the construction site starting and running for a short time.

The police interviewed the employees of the construction company and a search of the site determined the noises were not related to the disappearance of Jimmy Hoffa.

Another of the more colorful reports which came from a reputed mobster was that Jimmy had decided to end his career in the Teamsters Union and had run off to Brazil with a "go-go dancer." The rumor is not clear if it is Brazil, South America or Brazil, Indiana where Jimmy was born.

A member of the Teamsters claimed he saw Jimmy Hoffa wearing glasses, and checking into a motel three days after his disappearance. He checked in under the last name Jewell.

Another confession came from convicted murderer Ricky Powell. He claimed he dumped Hoffa's body in 30 feet of water in the Au Sable River in northern Lower Michigan. The river, considered one of the best brown trout fisheries east of the Rockies, runs about 138 miles in length from Frederic Township in Crawford county to Oscoda, Michigan where it empties into Lake Huron. Boating Magazine jumped on the story and offered $10,000 to anyone who could find the body. So far no one has claimed the reward.

An interesting, and possibly factual, account of where Jimmy Hoffa disappeared has a mob connection. It is rumored that he was murdered and disposed of in a "mob run" Detroit area meat rendering plant.

If one had to dispose of a body they never wanted found a rendering plant would be the ideal method.

Great Lakes Cold Case Files.......................................

Rendering plants are found all over the United States. It is where dead animals are "recycled." The rendering process involves grinding and cooking the carcasses of dead farm animals, the heads and hoofs of animals after they are butchered, deer and other wildlife killed along the roads we drive, and even sometimes our beloved pets.

The animals are first put through a machine that grinds them into small pieces. The parts are then cooked at a high temperature. As the meat is melted away from the bones it rises to the surface in a layer of yellow fat called tallow.

The meat and bones remaining in the vat are moved to a press where the remaining fat is squeezed out and the bones and meat are dried and ground into a gritty powder called bone meal.

The tallow and bone meal is mixed with other ingredients as a source of protein in the diets of poultry and swine and in pet foods. The animal fat is also used in animal feeds as an energy source.

While the rendering plant sounds disgusting to most, if they did not exist our cities would be plagued with disease from rotting carcasses.

It is also a very good way to dispose of a human body you never want to be found. The rendering plant where some say Jimmy Hoffa was ground up and melted down was later destroyed by fire.

Savannah, Georgia also made the list of possible resting places of Jimmy Hoffa. It is alleged that he is buried in the thick concrete of the helicopter pad of the Sheraton Savannah Resort Hotel.

An alleged mafia heavy weight, Raffaele Quasarano also known as "Jimmy Q" owned Central Sanitation Services in Hamtramck, Michigan which had a steel compacter used to crush junk cars. It is said that Jimmy Hoffa's body was in the trunk of one of the cars that was crushed into a dense solid cube of metal.

The Central Sanitation Services facility was also destroyed by fire in 1978. Ironically the Wayne County Jail is now built on the site.

There have been a few alleged mafia hit men who have confessed to either killing or being involved in the death of Jimmy Hoffa.

The 2004 book, *I Heard You Paint Houses,* by Charles Brandt, a former prosecutor and Chief Deputy Attorney General for the state of Delaware has a theory on Hoffa's death and disposal. The author says a retired Teamster, Hoffa friend, and admitted mafia hit man, Frank Sheeran, confessed to him about killing Hoffa.

Sheeran out of guilt confessed to Brandt that it was he who lured Hoffa to a meeting in Bloomfield Hills then drove him to a house in northwest

Detroit. There Sheeran says he shot Hoffa twice behind the ear then left the house. Hoffa's body laid dead on the floor for someone else to clean up.

In a later confession, Sheeran added that Hoffa's body was moved from the house in Detroit and taken to the Grand Lawn Cemetery, just minutes away, where it was cremated within an hour of his death.

Previously a rumor involving Sheeran resulted with the F.B.I. searching Sheeran's backyard looking for a buried briefcase that might have contained a syringe used to sedate Hoffa before he was killed. Nothing was found.

Donald "Tony the Greek" George Frankos, an admitted former mob hit man who became a state witness and testified against many mafia figures alleged in a Playboy Magazine article that he, John Sullivan and James Coonan had shot and cut up Jimmy Hoffa. He claimed that the pieces were put in an oil drum and buried beneath the field of the Giants Football Stadium in East Rutherford during its construction.

The F.B.I. declined to search the field feeling that the confession was not credible. However in 2003, before the stadium was torn down, Adam Savage and Jamie Hyneman from the television show "Mythbusters" used ground-penetrating radar to look deep under the playing surface at spots where it was reported Hoffa was buried, such as each end zone, the 50 yard line and the 10 yard line. The "Mythbusters" did not find any evidence that the ground below showed any disturbance…. "Myth Busted!"

Another reputed mobster was said to be involved in the Hoffa disappearance, Louie Milito. In 2006, Milito's wife Linda, claimed that Louie had told her that he killed the Teamster Union ex-president and dumped the body near the Staten Island's Verrazano-Narrows Bridge in New York City.

Still another alleged hit man, Richard "Iceman" Koklinski confessed he was one of five men who abducted and killed Jimmy Hoffa. This confession was made to the author of the 2006 book, *The Iceman; Confessions of a Mafia Contract Killer,* Philip Carlo.

Mythbusters used ground penetrating radar to look beneath Giant Stadium.

Authorities doubt the validity of the claim, due to the Iceman's previous confessions to murders that evidence proved he had not committed.

In 2003 the authorities drove up I-75 from Detroit to Bay City, Michigan to investigate what they termed a credible lead. They dug up a backyard where Hoffa was said to be buried under an above ground swimming pool. Their efforts turned up nothing.

In the same year, the yard of a private dwelling was dug up in Munger Township, located southeast of Bay City. Again nothing of interest was found.

Other rumors say; Hoffa's body was said to be stuffed into a 55-gallon oil drum and trucked to the Gulf of Mexico where the drum was dropped to the bottom of the Gulf.

In a 1982 U.S. Senate hearing, a federal witness testified that Hoffa had been chopped into small pieces, transported to Florida where he was dumped in a swamp as alligator food.

Another theory was that the Teamster was buried in a vacant field in Waterford Township in Oakland County.

It's said that a trash incinerator at the Central Waste Management company in Hamtramck, Michigan which was owned by two men who were reputed to have mob ties, was used to cremate Jimmy Hoffa.

It was also reported that the body was disposed of beneath a swimming pool at a mansion in Bloomfield Hills near Turtle Lake.

Cadillac, Michigan, located in the middle of the Lower Peninsula was also brought under scrutiny when a report surfaced that the remains of Jimmy Hoffa were buried under a public works garage.

Northwest of Detroit, in Highland, Michigan a 100-acre gravel pit was suspected of holding the answer of where the body of Jimmy Hoffa laid. A military airplane using high tech infra-red photography surveyed the area looking for a body but nothing was discovered.

In 2006, an article in the *Detroit News* reported that an inmate, Donovan Wells, incarcerated in the Federal Medical Center in Lexington, Kentucky wanted to trade information on Hoffa's disappearance in exchange for a reduced prison sentence he was serving for using his trucking company to transport marijuana from Texas to Detroit.

The information Mr. Wells provided led the Federal Bureau of Investigation to an 85-acre farm near Milford, Michigan where they dug in various locations on the farm for 13 days. A large barn on the property was torn down to assist in the search for the remains of Jimmy Hoffa.

A news helicopter flying over the farm filming the newest Hoffa search took photographs that appeared to indicate agents removing something from the ground. However, the F.B.I. never made a public press release indicating they found the remains of Jimmy Hoffa nor did they say that the search that cost taxpayers millions of dollars, was another bust.

Other theories of where Jimmy Hoffa has been for the past several decades include:

He is buried under a section of the New Jersey Turnpike.

He is encased in concrete near the Mackinaw Bridge that connects the Upper and Lower Peninsulas of Michigan.

He is buried in the yard of a home in Hamilton, New Jersey.

He was transported across the border to Toronto, Canada and buried in the Mondo Condo.

He is buried in the concrete foundation of Detroit's Renaissance Center.

He was cremated at the Wayne State University Medical School in Detroit.

Hoffa's body is being held in the United States Bullion Depository at Fort Knox.

And there is always the rumor that he is healthy, safe and living the good life in the United States Witness Protection Program.

A New Theory

In a July 1, 2007 article in the *Detroit Free Press*, staff writer Joel Thurtell reported a new theory as to why Jimmy Hoffa disappeared. While there is no definitive collaborating evidence to sustain the theory, there is substantial circumstantial evidence to make the theory interesting.

His claim is that Jimmy R. Hoffa, former President of the International Brotherhood of Teamsters, was killed by government agents.

He wrote that people in a position to know suggested Hoffa was killed by government agents to keep him from testifying at a House Select Committee on assassinations. He was preparing to tell all he knew about government-sanctioned assassinations with mafia involvement.

Possibly the long standing rumor of organized crime being responsible for high profile assassinations is true. Could this be a J.F.K. connection?

Jimmy Hoffa was a colorful character that exploded on the labor relations scene during the infancy of the movement.

Through cunning and bare knuckle brawling, Hoffa battled his way from the Kroger Grocery loading docks to be the president of the largest labor union in the world.

Its been said he could never have accomplished what he did if he had not, at times, partnered with some shady characters. It might have been this relationship with members of the mafia that is responsible for his disappearance and suspected murder.

Hoffa despised the cozy relationship organized crime had developed with the union and the influence it exercised on the Teamsters pension fund. He wanted to regain the presidency of the International Union and publicly vowed to clean house.

Who is directly responsible for abducting and possibly killing Jimmy Hoffa may never be known for sure, after all Jimmy Hoffa disappeared almost forty years ago and most of the persons who participated have passed on. What ultimately happened with the remains of Jimmy Hoffa is another mystery that may never be solved. Too many years have passed and too many false leads have surfaced. But each year or two another theory of what happened to Hoffa comes to light and starts a feeding frenzy of reporters rehashing all of the details of Jimmy Hoffa's rise to power in the Teamsters, his ruling of the Teamsters with an iron fist, his imprisonment for jury tampering, the mystery of his disappearance and of course, the ultimate question; What happened to Jimmy Hoffa?

The mystery surrounding Jimmy Hoffa again surfaced in the fall of 2012. When an unidentified elderly, man diagnosed with terminal cancer, told authorities of being present when a body was buried beneath the dirt floor of a storage shed at a Roseville, Michigan home. He said he had not told anyone of what he observed 37 years ago out of fear for his life and family.

He couldn't say with certainty it was the body of the labor leader, but it was possible because it occurred the day of or the day after the disappearance and the man who owned the house at the time was known to have ties with Detroit organized crime. The authorities took a cautious approach and said they were investigating a possible crime, not necessarily the disappearance of Hoffa.

In the years since the 1975 disappearance the shed floor had been paved over so ground-penetrating radar was brought in to peer below the concrete. The radar revealed the soil had indeed been disturbed. A section of the concrete was removed and soil samples were taken to be tested for evidence of human remains by a Michigan State University forensic anthropologist.

News reporters from across the nation covered the possible Hoffa discovery, the Hoffa mystery had not lost its intrigue. On October 2, 2012 the announcement was made to those anxiously awaiting the results that the soil samples taken from beneath the floor of the storage shed of the Florida Street home in Roseville, Michigan did not contain DNA evidence of Jimmy Hoffa, nor did contain evidence of any human remains.

It was just another high profile and expensive wild goose chase.

With Honesty He Lived;
For Honesty He Was Taken

Inscription on the tombstone of Senator Warren Hooper

In the short 40-year life of Warren Hooper, he accomplished many things. He attended college in California and Indiana, shipped out with the Merchant Marines taking him to exotic ports in Central and South America, and exciting cities in England and France. He became an investment broker and a member of the California Stock Exchange. He worked at newspapers in Tacoma and Seattle, Washington, and in Chicago, Illinois, Milwaukee, Wisconsin and Traverse City, Michigan.

In 1934 he entered Albion College in Albion, Michigan. While there he began working as a student for the local newspaper, the *Albion Evening Recorder*. In 1935 Mr. Hooper married Callienetta Cobb whom he met in college and he began working full time on the *Evening Recorder*.

A year later he left the *Albion Evening Recorder* to travel to Berlin, Germany to cover the 1936 Olympic games as a freelance reporter, writing articles for several magazines and newspapers.

Upon his return he and his wife operated a grocery and coal cooperative out of their home. In yet another career move a year later he started managing an automobile service station.

In 1938 Mr. Hooper, with the urging of working men he met through his grocery and gas

Senator Warren Green Hooper

station, registered as a Republican candidate for the State Legislature representing Eastern Calhoun County. He was sworn into the Michigan Legislature at Lansing in January 1939. Although just a freshman, Representative Hooper was selected by the Speaker of the House to chair the House Committee on Public Health.

Under his leadership the committee introduced bills to the House that would lay the groundwork for group hospital and medical plans.

Representative Hooper was selected over several candidates to be appointed the Executive Secretary of the Michigan Osteopathic Physicians and Surgeons Association; a position many felt was a conflict of interest for a sitting member of the legislature.

In 1944, when the state senator representing the 9th District stepped down from office, Representative Hooper entered the election to fill the senate seat. Despite being challenged by a popular Republican, Hooper won the party's nomination and won the senate seat. He was sworn into the Michigan Senate in 1944 at the state capital.

On January 11, 1945 about 3:00 PM, when the senate adjourned for the weekend, Senator Warren G. Hooper left the senate chambers and was approached by two men, one tall and thin with a dark overcoat. The senator seemed to know the man. The other man was introduced to the senator. He was short and stout wearing a light colored overcoat and a felt hat.

The conversation between the three men lasted about three minutes, then they departed. The identity of the men was not known. The senator went to the coatroom in the capitol building as he left for the weekend.

Dan Copeland, the coatroom attendant held his coat as Senator Hooper slid his arms in. In their conversation, Senator Hooper told Copeland that he would not be attending the Republican State Convention in Grand Rapids, rather he was going home to Albion where he had other matters to attend to.

The coatroom attendant watched Senator Hooper as he walked out to his car parked in the Capital drive.

The senator drove from the Capitol to McLaughlin Hospital where he had spent the last two nights in the residence of Dr. Lawrence Jarrett. From there he went to the Hotel Porter where Senator Hooper talked with the desk clerk about a room, the state convention of the Michigan Osteopathic Association was being held in Lansing that weekend. The desk clerk said Senator Hooper left shortly after 4:00 PM.

Prior to the senator arriving at the hotel, the desk clerk said a tall thin man and a short stout man had been at the hotel.

VOTE FOR

HOOPER

For State Senator

REPUBLICAN

Hooper campaign poster. Courtesy of Frank Passic, Albion Historian.

The 38-mile drive from the State's Capitol in Lansing to the town of Albion, the Senator's home, would take the senator a little less than an hour providing the day's snow had been plowed from the roads. He would drive down the two lane state highway, M-99, from the capitol though the cities of Eaton Rapids and Springport then on to Albion. But on that snowy Thursday, January 11, 1945 evening Senator Warren G. Hooper would not arrive in Albion, he would not be welcomed home by his wife and two young sons. He was found in his car along the side of M-99 with two .38 caliber bullets in his head.

On that evening, Floyd Modjeska, a grain elevator operator from Springport was driving along M-99 and noticed that smoke was coming from a car parked on the left side of the road. He stopped and as he walked towards the car he noticed a bullet hole in the right rear window. He looked into the interior of the car but could not see anyone inside due to the dense smoke.

He waved down another passing car, driven by Kyle Van Auker of Eaton Rapids and fifteen minutes later M. D. Howard from Lansing happened along M-99 and saw the smoke and the men peering into the vehicle.

The car emitting the smoke was parked on the left shoulder, the wrong side of the road for a car driving south, the ignition was turned off and the transmission in neutral.

The men stood around the car and some women from a local farm came along. The women urged the men to move away for fear the car was going to explode but the men calmed their fears. It was not until Modjeska noticed a foot at the floor of the car that the men opted to open the door and examine the interior of the vehicle.

The men opened the door and the smoldering fire, apparently starving for lack of oxygen, burst into flames.

As the smoke billowed from the car, it became apparent a body was slumped on the right side of the front seat. Its head towards the steering wheel and legs sprawled in front of it.

The men dragged the burning body out of the car onto the pavement and threw snow into the car to put out the flaming seat cushion. They also threw snow on the body to extinguish the flames, but the side of the body had been badly burned.

Police were called and the body found in the smoldering car was identified as that of Warren G. Hooper, Michigan State Senator from the 9th district, an office he had held for only two weeks.

The police observed footprints in the snow leading from the left side, driver's side, of the car walking towards the pavement of M-99. They looked as though a pair of low flat shoes had made them. The prints were small, the police theorized, made by a woman or a small man.

The State Police asked the county Sheriff's department to notify Mrs. Hooper about the death of her husband. Deputy George Lewis went to the Hooper house but the family was not in. When Mrs. Hooper and her two sons, age 4 and 6, returned from having dinner at a local restaurant, Deputy Lewis told her the bad news.

Mrs. Hooper went with the deputy to the Sheriff's office in Springport and was briefly interviewed to see if she could shed any light on the murder of the senator.

The recent widow told them she had received two suspicious telephone calls that day. Mrs. Hooper said she did not recognize the caller, and the man refused to identify himself. The caller asked when the senator was expected home and how he was traveling.

Mrs. Hopper told the deputy that Senator Hooper's Albion secretary, Agnes Wickens, was helping out in the Lansing office that week and was scheduled to ride back to Albion with him on Thursday.

Her body was not found in the car on M-99. The police theorized that possibly the people who had killed the senator had abducted her. There were a few tense hours before Mrs. Wickens was located; she had decided to remain in Lansing for the weekend.

At the scene of the murder, the investigators determined the senator's car had been forced off the road and came to a skidding stop on the left side gravel shoulder. Furthermore, from the evidence observed in the car, they decided the fatal shots were fired from someone within the automobile or someone reaching inside the window.

The car was towed to the Jackson State Police post where a team of investigators scoured it for evidence that might have been left behind during the murder. Senator Hooper's body was taken to Lansing for an autopsy.

Investigators surmised the car was not intentionally set on fire, rather Senator Hooper was probably smoking a cigarette at the time he was fatally shot and the cigarette fell to the cushion, igniting it.

Dr. Charles Black, Lansing Pathologist and Dr. Charles Muehlberger, director of the State Crime Laboratory performed the autopsy on the senator. They reported that the Senator had been shot two times with a .38 caliber pistol. The powder burns on his head and hat indicate the shots were fired at point blank range.

One bullet struck the senator below his left eye coming to rest in his right side of his throat. Another bullet entered the top of his head and stopped under his right shoulder blade. The investigation further revealed that a third bullet missed Senator Hooper and went through the rear window. The doctors who preformed the autopsy said either of the bullets that struck the senator could have killed him.

The senator's body had been severely burned by the flaming cushion from his knees to his chest.

The State Police and local authorities requested the newspapers and radio stations to announce their need for assistance.

Had anyone seen strangers on M-99 about the time of the murder? Possibly the murder had been a robbery that had gone terribly wrong by an indigent hitchhiker. Or could there have been an assassin posing as a hitchhiker?

The authorities wanted to know if anyone had seen cars stopped along the road, strangers in the area acting suspicious, or anything at all unusual.

A lead came in from two county snowplow operators, Ben Wright and Harold Peterson. They both reported seeing a maroon colored sedan with three men traveling at a high rate of speed. The car was observed about 5:20 PM driving away from the area heading in the direction of Jackson, Michigan.

Based on the fact that the three men discovered Senator Hooper's car at 5:30 PM, and the maroon car, if it indeed was involved, was sighted at 5:20 led the police to believe the murder was committed between 5:00 and 5:15 PM.

The assassination of the State of Michigan Senator was not taken lightly. The murder became one of the most intensive investigations in the history of the Michigan State Police.

Governor Kelly announced at the State Republican Convention in Grand Rapids that he would throw the full police resources of the state into the investigation.

The State police set up a temporary headquarters in Jackson, Michigan and formed a team of investigators under the direction of Lieutenant Lyle Morse. He had seven Michigan State Police detectives dedicated to the case, and literally hundreds of police and deputies at his disposal.

The police drew law enforcement agencies from other states into the investigation on the possibility that the senator's death was the result of a professional murderer. Known professionals from around the nation were picked up and interrogated as to where they were on January 11, 1945.

The *Detroit News* offered a reward of $5,000.00 for the apprehension and conviction of the person or persons responsible for the murder of Senator Hooper. The legislature a few days later approved a bill offering a $25,000.00 reward.

The chance at $30,000 brought in hundreds of tips. Some were quite fanciful and others were credible enough to investigate.

One tip that was given to a newspaper reporter claimed that Detroit's notorious Purple Gang was involved.

Other people called in that they had seen a car parked on the side of M-99 around 2:30 PM, about one and a half miles south of Eaton Rapids on the day of the killing.

The car was observed sitting at the side of the road for approximately 30 minutes while the men worked at the rear of the car, as if they were putting on the license plate. They then got back in the car and proceeded down M-99 towards the location where the Senator was later found.

The authorities were developing a list of possible motives for the murder of the Michigan State Senator. Could it have been a random act of violence along the desolate stretch of road? Could it have had anything to do with legislation the senator was working on? It could have been robbery but the senator only had two one-dollar bills, some change, a pocket watch and ring with him and they remained on the body. His small overnight bag containing a pair of pajamas and toiletries looked undisturbed.

The strongest motive for the assassination of the senator could not be overlooked. The Monday following his murder, Senator Warren Hooper was going to testify at a grand jury about corruption in state government.

In the mid 1940s, corruption ran rampant at every level of state government. It was a well-known fact that legislation was often influenced by bribery. A few hundred dollars given to a senator or state representative to vote in favor of a bill or to not vote for a bill was commonplace.

The corruption was widely accepted as the way of doing business... but not by all. There were a growing number of people who wanted to clean up Michigan government.

One person who was taking a lead in cleaning up the government was Judge Leland W. Carr. The judge was the chairman of a one-man Grand Jury investigating graft and the bribery of state representatives and senators.

The judge assigned Kim Sigler as the Special prosecutor of the grand jury.

For more than two years Mr. Sigler and a team of investigators worked on the project, finally naming over 50 prominent men including many representatives and senators in warrants. Twenty of them had been convicted of crimes related to bribery; sixteen were appealing their convictions and others were awaiting their trials.

The death of Senator Warren G. Hooper came as quite a blow to the case Mr. Sigler was preparing. The prosecutor reported in the *Lansing State Journal* that Senator Hooper was going to be a major witness against three men involving bribery and attempted bribery of government officials.

Great Lakes Cold Case Files..

The men were Frank McKay, Floyd Fitzsimmons, and William Green. They had an interest in a bill that had gone before the Michigan legislature that would allow para-mutual betting at horse racing tracks around the state.

Frank McKay, from Grand Rapids, Michigan, was a very prominent man within the Republican Party on both the state and national levels. He was known as a political boss in Michigan, a position he held for decades.

McKay had been the subject of a grand jury investigation in 1931 as the result of his use of state funds when he was treasurer. He was also named in three other grand juries for alleged allegations of fraud, kickbacks and extortion.

Floyd Fitzsimmons was a sports promoter from Benton Harbor and Green was a former state representative from Hillman, Michigan.

Senator Hooper admitted that he had accepted a bribe while he was a member of the House of Representatives but was granted immunity in exchange for his testimony in the grand jury probe of the three men and of William J. Burns, the Executive Secretary of the Michigan Medical Society, also being investigated for bribing elected officials for their favorable vote on medical legislation.

The tip provided earlier in the investigation about members of the Detroit's notorious Purple Gang possibly being responsible for the assassination of Senator Hooper might not have been as far fetched as it originally seemed.

The tipster said he had seen a member of the Purple Gang who had relatives in Albion. The police discounted the tip, since the mobster was doing time in Jackson Prison at the time of the murder.

Detroit's Purple Gang was one of the most feared gangs in the nation during the mid 1920s and early 1930s, well known for their brutality and the violent deaths that followed in their wake.

The gang began as a group of juvenile delinquent Jewish teenagers who shoplifted and harassed shopkeepers in their neighborhood.

Members of Detroit's notorious Purple Gang.

They reportedly got their name from a shopkeeper who said the boys were rotten, rotten purple like the color of rancid meat.

Prohibition, the federal government's ban on manufacturing, purchasing, possessing or consuming alcoholic beverages was in effect during the rise of the Purple Gang and the teenage thugs graduated from being pesky hoodlums into hardened murderous mobsters engaged in armed robbery, hijacking, extortion and murder.

During prohibition, most of the illegal beer, gin, rum and whiskey that entered the United States came across the Detroit River that separates the U.S. and Canada. The distillers and breweries of Canada readily sold their products by the boatload to vessels that held a bill of lading showing the cargo they were buying was destined for somewhere in the Caribbean where it was legal.

But the same boat and crew would show up at the distillery dock on the Detroit River the very next day for another cargo of booze to deliver to Jamaica or the Bahamas.

The trip across the river by boat, or in the winter over the river's ice, to docks piled high with cases of Canadian beer and booze was a trip often made.

The Purple Gang was not known to make many runs across the river; they found it easier and more profitable to heist the illegal cargo from the bootleggers once it was on U.S. soil. They would steal the booze as it was being off loaded at the river's edge or hijack the delivery trucks once the cargo was loaded.

The bootleggers needed to carry weapons and be ready to use them because the Purple Gang was quick to use theirs when stealing the illegal cargo. The police estimated the Purple Gang was responsible for at least 500 unsolved murders through a five-year period during the prohibition years. The police were not too concerned about the bodies of the dead bootleggers piling up. They considered it just criminals killing other criminals.

The Purple Gang was once so powerful that Al Capone, the undisputed boss of Chicago's underworld, chose to buy booze from the Detroit gangsters rather than to move in on their territory. Capone thought an attempt to take over the Detroit illegal booze market from the Purple Gang would result in a bloodbath of epic proportions.

In the 1930s, the Purple Gang began to lose their power in the Detroit underworld. Several of the high ranking gang leaders were serving long prison terms for their crimes, and the remaining members began to bicker and their inter-gang fighting eventually made Detroit an easy and profitable target for the mafia under Joe Zerilli.

The relationship between the Purple Gang and Albion, the city Senator Hooper had called home for a decade, goes deeper than a tipster trying to cash in on a $30,000 reward. As the power of the Purple Gang subsided in Detroit, some members of the gang that were not incarcerated or dead moved to Albion.

When leaders Raymond Bernstein and Harry Keywell were sent away in 1931 for murder; Harry Fleisher became a leader of the gang. Harry's brothers, Louis and Sam, both respected leaders of the gang moved out of Detroit in 1935 and purchased a junkyard, The Riverside Iron and Metal Company, in Albion with another gang member, Sam Bernstein.

They continued their criminal activities using the junkyard as their headquarters.

Many mobsters were said to have stopped off in Albion as they traveled between Detroit and Chicago. In Albion they visited the Street Car Tavern, owned by Purple Gang members and stayed at a hotel also owned by members of the gang.

During this time there was a series of safe robberies in the southwest Michigan area. Banks and stores in Jackson, Albion, Battle Creek, Coldwater, Ionia, Grand Rapids and Lansing were the targets of unknown thieves. Sometimes the safe was blown open and other times the entire safe was rolled out of the store and driven away.

In 1936, a police raid on the junkyard and an Albion garage ended with the arrest of Louis Fleisher and his wife Nelli and Sam and Lillian Bernstein.

Police displaying the Graham-Paige sedan used by members of the Purple Gang to crack safes. Courtesy of Frank Passic, Albion Historian, from the book "Albion in the 20th Century."

The car they were using to rob the safes, a gun-metal-colored, armor-plated Graham-Paige sedan, was found stored in the Albion parking garage. The State Police called it a perfect vehicle for safe robberies. The windows were three quarters of an inch thick, there were heavy steel plates welded on the car to protect the tires, passengers and other vital parts of the car from gunfire. The car had a removable back seat so a safe could be carried and the car held a long list of safe cracking tools including nitro-glycerin, wires and dynamite. In addition the car contained two rifles, two sawed-off shotguns, three revolvers and two automatic pistols, the police noted it even contained a handcart to wheel a safe out of a building to the car.

The prosecutor felt he had a solid case against Harry Fleisher and Sam Bernstein but the two mobsters were eventually released for lack of evidence.

The investigation into the senator's assassination took an interesting turn when an ex-convict from Jackson Prison told Attorney General John R. Dethmers that he had been propositioned to kill Senator Hooper.

The Attorney General was investigating abnormalities at Jackson State Prison, which in 1945 was the largest walled-prison in the world.

Dethmers turned the tip over to authorities that were investigating the senator's murder.

The ex-con, Henry Luks, said while he was in Jackson State Prison he was approached by Henry Fleisher and Mike Selik and offered $5,000 to kill Warren Hooper.

They originally suggested that the senator's car be wired with dynamite and blown up. But when dynamite wasn't readily available, other means of doing away with Hooper were discussed.

Luks told authorities he and another prisoner, Sam Abramowicz, were allowed to leave the prison with Henry Fleisher and Selik, known gangsters, on two occasions and driven to Albion. The two convicts said Selik gave them a .38 caliber pistol for them to use on the senator.

However the senator could not be located and the assassination did not happen.

The fact that the prisoners were allowed to leave the prison and other unusual occurrences at Jackson State Prison led to a scandal at the prison that resulted in seven of the top administrators being suspended and many other prison employees under investigation.

As Attorney General Dethmers said after a four month long investigation, he found the prison was being ruled by a ring of big time convicts that had their own way within the prison walls and could come and go almost whenever they wanted.

Known gangsters were permitted to privately meet with convicts inside the prison and inmates were given furloughs from the prison yet prison paperwork was fudged to show them still on the count as present.

Vice and gambling also ran rampant in the prison while some guards and officers turned a closed eye to it. Some officers even took inmates by car to local houses of prostitution and to their own homes for parties where the inmates were served alcoholic beverages.

Two ex-cons who were serving time in the prison but allowed to leave with two known gangsters on a mission to assassinate a senator later turned state's witnesses told of the lack of control the prison administration exercised.

Special Prosecutor Kim Sigler could not prove who had killed Senator Hooper to silence him but he thought he could prove a case against four men who he felt conspired to kill the senator.

On July 16, 1945, the conspiracy to commit murder trial began. The prosecutor brought charges against four men; Harry Fleisher, a former leader in the notorious Purple Gang, Sam Fleisher, another Purple Gang mobster,

Witnesses Hunted By Detectives in Murder of Hooper

Sigler Says Identities Of the Pair Believed Known

ONE MAN TALL, OTHER SHORT

Myron "Mike" Selik, a man with Purple Gang connections and Pete Mahoney, Harry Fleisher's best friend and fellow mobster.

The State had witnesses, who stated under oath, the four men had indeed plotted to kill the senator before he had an opportunity to testify before Judge Carr's Grand Jury.

The witnesses included the two Jackson Prison inmates, Sam Abramowicz and Harry Luks who agreed to kill he senator but did not accomplish it, Al Kurner another Jackson Prison inmate who said he too had been approached to murder Mr. Hooper, Jeanette Welker a former girlfriend of Harry Fleisher and Evelyn Brown, the manager of the Top Hat Tavern in Albion, Michigan who testified that she observed Pete Mahoney with another man, Harry Fleisher, in Albion in the tavern on the day of the senator's murder.

The men were found guilty of conspiring to kill Senator Hooper and received the maximum sentence for the crime, four and half to five years in prison. However, no one was ever convicted of the brutal murder of a seated State Senator nor was the person who put up the money for the killing ever indicted, brought to trial or named.

Senator Warren Green Hooper did not die for naught. The men he was going to testify against, Frank McKay, Floyd Fitzsimmons, and William

Green were found not guilty of bribing legislators for their votes on a Para mutual betting bill, and the senator's death brought to light the enormity of the problem of corruption in Michigan government.

Judge Carr's grand jury eventually issued 1300 subpoenas, which resulted in 130 arrests. There were 62 convictions that included a former attorney general, 23 state legislators and more than thirty other government employees.

Another outcome of the senator's death was the house cleaning at Jackson Prison that ended the corruption that permeated the walls of the world's largest wall-prison.

As a side note: In the 1946 election Special Prosecutor Kim Sigler was elected the governor of Michigan. Both Judge Leland Carr and Attorney General John Dethmers were appointed to the Michigan Supreme Court.

The Mad Butcher Of Kingsbury Run

Remember being young and walking home from school on a warm fall day? Ambling along in no hurry, maybe kicking a rock, or taking a short cut through a field, walking along a creek looking through the garbage strewn about for treasures that you could use to build a clubhouse. Those were the days of innocence for most kids. But, on a September day of 1935 in the bushes of Kingsbury Run two boys walking home from school found more than they expected, they found the decaying, headless body of a man.

There was an area of Cleveland, Ohio called the Kingsbury Run. It is a riverbed dried up for centuries that formed a depression in the topography of the city. Since the land was rugged and unusable, it became an eyesore for the city. Refuse was thrown about, houses hastily built by squatters not following building codes, and the people of the dregs of society populated Kingsbury Run. Homeless men, out of work and out of luck huddled around fires for warmth. The buildings that were in the area were saloons, brothels and a few factory buildings from the previous century now left to decay. The "Run" was not a hospitable place.

The Cleveland Police arrived at Kingsbury Run responding to a call that there was a dead body discovered. The body was of a young white male. His head and penis had been removed. The police cordoned off the area to look for the missing body parts.

In their search, they discovered another body, again missing his head and penis. This body showed obvious signs of decay. It had been killed several weeks earlier.

The men's penises were found laying nearby as if the killer had tossed them aside and the heads were found partially buried.

Once removed to the coroner's office, it was determined that the first body found was of a younger man and he had been dead about three days. Fingerprints taken from the body revealed it was the remains of Edward Andrassy, a 28-year-old small time criminal from the Kingsbury Run area.

145

The absence of blood in the soil beneath the men as they laid in the "Run," indicated the men had been killed somewhere else, washed clean and left there. The murderer took the time to pose both corpses. They were lying on their backs, legs spread and arms positioned along their sides. The second body discovered was that of an older man who had been dead for up to three weeks. Since he was in a state of advanced decomposition, fingerprints could not be used for identification. The pathologist was puzzled about the discoloration on the torso of the body. It appeared as though the killer had tried to use some chemical to retard the decomposition. It had not worked.

Both men had died as a result of decapitation. They were tied at the wrists and feet. The ligature marks on their limbs showed the men had struggled as the murderer methodically sliced through the flesh of their throats, cut their jugular vein and drained their bodies of life giving blood. Because of the skill displayed the police deduced the murderer might be from the medical field. The decapitation showed signs of medical training. Possibly the killer had gained his knowledge through an occupation such as a butcher.

The police investigated the murders. They talked to known criminals and prostitutes since Andrassy associated with people from that life. While they found some who wished him dead, they didn't find any leads in his death.

Four months later, in January 1936, a howling dog caught the attention of a woman. She found the chained dog barking and trying to get at a basket. With a quick look into the burlap bag in the basket she told a neighbor that it had hams in it. The neighbor looked and corrected her. It was an arm, a human arm.

The burlap bag contained the body of a woman. Her head, left arm and both legs had been removed.

POLICE BAFFLED AT CLEVELAND IN TORSO SLAYINGS

Nine Victims of Mysterious Killer Within a Period of Two Years.

BY DAVID I. RIMMEL.

Copyright by the NANA (The Lincoln Journal and other newspapers).

CLEVELAND —At the close of two years' investigation into the growing list of Cleveland torso slayings, called the "Kingsbury Run murders" after the section of the city in which the butchered remains of most of the nine victims have been disposed, homicide investigators are still without clues to the motives and identity of the killer who is creating one of the most weird chains of death in modern crime history.

Fingerprinting the right hand of the corpse identified it as belonging to Florence Polillo. "Flo," described as an overweight and unattractive, aging prostitute, was well known in the areas bars.

A few weeks later, Flo's left arm and the legs were discovered in the weeds of a vacant lot. Her head was never found.

The Cleveland Police searched for some connection between the murders. At first it looked as though the deaths of the two men, with their penises cut off was the work of a homosexual. But the murder of Flo didn't follow the pattern. She was female, she was a prostitute, her genitals had not been mutilated. The case perplexed the authorities.

To confound the investigation all the more, an officer remembered that two years prior a female torso that had been found floating in Lake Erie. Her legs were cut off at the knees, her head missing. She was in her twenties and like the second body found, a substance had been applied to her body in an effort to slow decomposition. The identification of the woman was never discovered. She was known only as the "Lady in the Lake."

It was in June of 1936 when the killer struck again.

Some young boys found a pair of men's trousers under a bridge in the Kingsbury Run. One can only imagine their shock and surprise when they found the pants were wrapping the decapitated head of a man. The headless torso was found a quarter of a mile away.

Torso Victim, Scene of Slaying

With the confession of Frank Dolezal, 52, to slaying and dismembering Mrs. Florence Polillo, one of Cleveland Ohio's, 12 torso murder victims, police officials renewed efforts to solve the other 11 cases. Photos above show—top, entrance to the murder house occupied by Dolezal. Lower left—Mrs. Polillo. Lower right—the bath tub in which Dolezal is accused of dismembering Mrs. Polillo.
—Central Press Photos.

From the blood soaked ground around the body it was obvious the man had been killed at that location. As with the other murders, the cause of death for this man was decapitation.

The man had several tattoos decorating

his body. His identification should easily be made from the identifiable body art but despite the police departments best efforts, the identity of the man was never made. He is referred to as the "Tattoo Man."

A young girl was walking in the Kingsbury Run when she happened upon the decomposing, headless body of a white male about forty years old. His head was found nearby along with a bloody pile of his clothes. By the amount of blood found in the ground, the man had been killed at that spot about two months earlier.

The next victim was found when a woman tripped over the upper half of a man's torso. The body had been sliced in half. The bottom half of the torso and parts of both legs were found in an open sewer.

The man, in his twenties, died instantly when his throat was cut through in one stroke. The coroner noted that the dismemberment and decapitation were done with the skill of a person who had knowledge of anatomy.

Cleveland in the mid 1930s was struggling with rampant crime. Gangsters, prostitution, and gambling were openly flourishing in the city. To combat the crime wave, the mayor and city council hired the most prominent lawman in the country. They hired Elliot Ness to be the new Director of Public Safety.

Ness had excelled at cleaning up organized crime in Chicago; he was the man who brought down Al Capone. Now he had the assignment of cleaning up Cleveland. He never expected to become immersed in a case involving a vicious serial killer.

In February 1937, the next body was

The Madman Who Has Committed 8 "Perfect Murders"

Mystery of the Killer of Kingsbury Run Who Cuts Off His Victim's Head With One Sweep of His Knife Through the Back of the Neck and Leaves No Clue

discovered. The upper half of a woman's torso was found washed up on the shore of Lake Erie. Her lower half came ashore about three months later. She had been decapitated, but unlike the previous victims, it was not the cause of death. Rather her head had been cut off after she was already dead.

A skull was found in June 1937. A bag containing the rest of the skeleton was later discovered. Through dental records, it was determined the skeleton was that of Rose Wallace, a black woman who lived in the Kingsbury Run area.

The ninth victim was a man in his mid to late thirties. His dismembered body was discovered in the Cuyahoga River. The stomach of the man had been gutted and his heart was ripped from the body. His head nor his identity were never found.

Victim number ten was also found in the Cuyahoga River. A man saw what he thought was a dead fish. It turned out to be the lower leg of a woman. Several weeks later, two burlap bags containing the woman's torso and parts of her legs were pulled from the river.

The coroner detected drugs in the system of the woman's body. She might have been drugged prior to her murder or she may have been a drug addict. If her arms had been found, the police might have discovered needle marks but they were never found.

In August 1938, three men scavenging for scrap metal in the garbage piles of Kingsbury Run made a grizzly discovery, the torso of a young woman. Her head, arms and legs surgically removed were found a few feet away wrapped in butcher's paper and hidden in a wood box. While the

Great Lakes Cold Case Files..........................

Wednesday Evening, August 17, 1938   THE ABILENE REPORTER-NEWS   PAGE THREE

BOTH UNIDENTIFIED WOMEN—

Bodies of Mad Torso Slayer's Eleventh and Twelfth Victims Found

PIECEMEAL DISCOVERIES SHOW
MURDERER'S SURGICAL SKILL

Detectives Spurred in Hunt for Fiend
Whose First Victim Found in Fall of '35

Cleveland Police were searching the area for any clues, they found body number 12. Another body was left just a few yards from number 11.

These two bodies were left in a location that is in view of the office window of Elliot Ness. It was as though the murderer was playing cat and mouse with the Cleveland Director of Public Safety.

The police had interviewed close to 5,000 people during their investigation. Most of the interviews led to nothing. Thousands of police hours were dedicated to the case with little to show for it. The killer had covered his tracks and managed to elude capture.

There was one man in which the police became very interested. The man had the medical knowledge the police suspected the killer had. He had grown up in Kingsbury Run and was well acquainted with the area. The Man was Dr. Frank Sweeney.

Dr. Sweeney was born of poor parents and lived in Kingsbury Run as a child. He was knowledgeable of the area, having spent years as a boy exploring and playing in the Run. Frank Sweeney was a medical doctor so he had the medical knowledge and he also had served in an army field hospital during World War I where one of his main duties was amputating the limbs of soldiers wounded in combat.

Dr. Sweeney was a brilliant man who rose far above his humble beginnings but had recently fallen victim to his own demons. He, as his father before him, was a raging alcoholic. Because of his inability to control his alcoholism, he was asked to leave the hospital, and his wife divorced him and the court barred him from seeing his children. This occurred about the time the Kingsbury Run killings began.

Since Dr. Sweeney was the cousin to Martin Sweeney, a congressman who was a very vocal opponent to the seated mayor, Elliot Ness's suspicions of the doctor were kept low key. Once he had gathered enough evidence to confirm his suspicion, the lawman invited the doctor to a local hotel to be interviewed. The hotel was selected over the police station so as not to arouse the throng of newsmen camped out on the police station front stairs, and so as not to excite Congressman Sweeney.

The doctor was interviewed by Elliot Ness to no conclusion. The doctor was then given a polygraph test. Polygraph tests in the 1930s were not an accepted practice, but Mr. Ness still had contacts in Chicago and brought one of the polygraph inventors to Cleveland to examine Dr. Sweeney.

Dr. Sweeny sat for two polygraph tests that day and in each instance the test indicated he was indeed the "Mad Butcher of Kingsbury Run."

Shortly after the interrogation and the lie detector tests, Dr. Sweeney checked himself into a hospital. From 1938 until 1965 when he died, Dr. Sweeney, remained in various hospitals. The doctor never admitted that he had killed and dismembered the twelve people found in Kingsbury Run, nor was the doctor ever arrested or convicted for the murders. But from the time of his hospitalization in 1938 after he met with Elliot Ness in the hotel, there were no more murders.

Cleveland hired the esteemed lawman, Elliot Ness, to clean up their city as he had done in Chicago, but he met his match with the "Mad Butcher of Kingsbury Run." The citizens of Cleveland were furious that their high priced Director of Public Safety could not uncover the identity of the killer. A few years later when Ness ran for mayor of Cleveland, he was soundly defeated.

The "Mad Butcher of Kingsbury Run" was officially responsible for decapitating and dismembering twelve people. Yet some believe that the headless bodies discovered in Pennsylvania and dismembered bodies found in New York State and in Ohio cities were the work of the butcher. Although

those murders were never officially credited to the Mad Butcher of Kingsbury Run, no other murderer was ever charged either.

One of the most infamous murderers in the annals of crime is London England's Jack the Ripper. The London police searched for a man who killed and dismembered street women. Jack the Ripper disemboweled his victims by surgically removing various organs from their bodies, demonstrating a certain amount of medical knowledge.

It is generally accepted that London's Jack the Ripper killed between five and seven women, while the "Mad Butcher of Kingsbury Run" killed and dismembered at least twelve, possibly more. The person responsible for the deaths in either case was never found. Could the murders that occurred on opposite sides of the Atlantic Ocean be related?

Beatings And Murder In Toledo, Ohio

On a mild spring evening, 48 year-old Emma Hatfield was walking to her home. As she walked through the darkness on the streets of Toledo, Ohio, a person dressed in dark clothes leapt from the shadows of an alley between Palmwood and Fernwood Avenues and struck her on the back of the head with a club.

The madman dragged the nearly unconscious woman down the alley, pausing to beat the woman and rip and cut articles of clothing from her body.

Dragged nearly 100 feet down the alley strewn with the garbage and filth of an urban city, the fiend continued to beat and cut the poor unconscious woman, then left her lying nude in a crimson pool of her own blood.

Mrs. Emma Hatfield's skull was fractured in several places, there were two gashes in her face, possibly caused by an axe, her body was covered with bruises and bleeding cuts. However, she was still alive. The poor battered woman laid unconscious in the hospital, ultimately dying from the beating months later.

Mrs. Hatfield's violent death was not an isolated occurrence, for in 1925 in Toledo, Ohio, a maniac was cruising the streets of Toledo beating and butchering women. Within a three mile range, twelve women were attacked, seven severely beaten and five died a violent death at the hands of a fiend who became known as the "Toledo Clubber."

The twelve attacks were all similar; a man dressed in dark clothing would usually hide behind a tree and when a woman walked by he would raise his club and lay a blow on the poor unsuspecting woman's head.

Mrs. Frank Hall was just a block from her Putnam Street home when a hand reached out from behind a tree, grabbed her hair and a club swung down striking her on the left temple. She fell to the ground, the grip on her hair slowing her descent while the club continued to land blows on her body.

SEARCH FOR TOLEDO CLUBBER BROADENS

Three Arrested While Rewards Have Increased To $12,200—Detroit Angle Investigated In Search For Fiend.

Mrs. Hall, despite being severely beaten, lived through the ordeal. But her doctor said her body would never recover from the beating nor would she psychologically recover from the horror of the event.

A twenty-four year-old mother of two, Lynda Baumgartner met the club wielding fiend on a dark night when his club struck out from behind a tree smashing into the left side of her head. Her unconscious body was dragged into the darkness where the maniac beat her lifeless body while ripping and cutting her clothing from her.

The murderer clubbed and slashed at the woman's body nearly completely severing Mrs. Baumgartner's head from her body.

The badly beaten corpse of 42 year old Mary Handley was found in the rear of the yard next to her own home. She had been struck with such force with a brick, the coroner said she died instantly. Then her dead body was dragged to the back yard, where the fiend continued to smash the brick into the woman's head. Her clothing was ripped and slashed with a knife leaving her almost completely nude. Some of Miss Handley's undergarments had been stuffed down her throat. Had she not died from the beating, she would have suffocated from her own underwear.

The Toledo police at first thought there were two monsters killing the women of Toledo; one who used a club to beat women and another who liked to slash them with a knife or axe. But they soon realized there was just one madman whose intent was to subject women to horribly violent deaths.

Various civic groups of Toledo offered a $12,200.00 reward for the arrest and conviction of the evil brute that was doing the murders. This brought in leads, some promising some not.

Three men were arrested as suspects in the crimes; a man was found lurking in the woods outside of Parma, Ohio. He was carrying a club. The second was a Detroit, Michigan man, said to be feeble minded, who was in Toledo the dates of two of the murders. His friends said when he returned, he had scratches on his arms and neck that looked like they were from a woman. And the third was never named but Toledo Police Chief Jennings said he was investigating a local man who by day was a respectable businessman but may be living a double life by night.

The police had scores of uniformed and undercover officers in street clothes patrolling the neighborhood where the attacks occurred, but despite

the vigilance of the police, the butcher attacked 30 year old Mrs. Frieda Draheim. She was one of the lucky ones, he beat her senseless but did not kill her. Twenty four hours later, while the police maintained their tight surveillance, the murderer again swung his club striking 38 year old Cora Bachlor. While recoiling from the initial blow she turned to see her attacker.

She said the man's face was distorted in perverse pleasure and laughing while Mrs. Bachlor pleaded for her life. When she started to scream, the monster fled.

Those suspects were able to prove their innocence and the police next theorized since the crime was so horrifically violent, the beast who was terrorizing the women of Toledo had to be a deranged person who lived on the lower fringes of society.

They rounded up all, "feeble minded, deranged and queer characters," of the city and questioned them. If they could produce a viable alibi for the time of the attacks they were released, if not they were either jailed or sent to the insane asylum.

The beatings and murders stopped. Had the police incarcerated the monster or scared him off?

The women of Toledo still lived in fear but the intensity quelled as the attacks stopped. Women began to walk the streets, visit friends and the police presence in the killing zone decreased.

There was little by way of clues to bring in the madman, he simply vanished, until the deranged assassin returned to slaughter another victim.

Pretty, twenty-six year old, Lily Croy was walking the two blocks from the University library to the Washington School where she lived and was a teacher.

As she walked on the Washington School campus in the darkness of the early evening, little did she know a sinister figure was hiding behind a tree her path would soon pass.

The madman suddenly stepped out from the shadows and brought his club heavily down on Miss Croy's head. The stunned girl was not immediately rendered unconscious and probably pleaded with her executioner, but he held a tight grip on her hair as he beat her.

The killer dragged the girl's limp body across the open grass lawn by the hair of her crushed skull to an area beneath a stairway of the school. The fiend then had the seclusion he desired.

In the shadows, he cut the clothes from her, removed her shoes and nylon hose revealing her naked dead body to his devious desires. Then he brutally beat the nude body of the young woman and slashed at it with a knife.

The severe beating and murder of the pretty school teacher renewed the horror that had earlier consumed Toledo, but it was the last of the violent murders. The madman who had terrorized the Ohio town slipped away into the night to never return. The beatings, slashing and murders had stopped.

No one was ever captured while in the process of beating a woman despite the intense police presence. No one was arrested for the murders. Almost 90 years after the last woman, Lily Croy, was beaten, stripped and slashed and left dead, the case of the Toledo Clubber remains open.

Someone Left Baby Nicole Outside To Die

On the night of December 26, 1989 a 10-month-old baby disappeared from her crib and was later found dead. The murderer of the child is still at large.

The police received a call informing them that a 10-month-old baby girl, Nicole Lee Hattamer, was missing from her Lake Holcombe, Wisconsin home. She had been last seen when the child was laid down for the night in her crib.

At home at the time of the disappearance were, the child's 17-year-old mother, grandparents, and the mother's younger brother and sister. Someone checked on the sleeping child and discovered baby Nicole was missing.

Nicole was much too young to get out of her crib, crawl to the door, open the door and crawl outside, so it was obvious another person was involved in her disappearance.

Firemen and other emergency responders from Chippewa County searched the snow-covered yard looking for evidence that someone entered or left the house after kidnapping the baby.

About 5:00 AM, six hours after the child went missing, one of the firemen alerted the others searching the grounds that he had located the child in the backyard. About 125 feet from the rear of the house, baby Nicole was lying face down in the snow.

An autopsy performed on the infant indicated she died either from freezing to death or by internal bleeding.

STATE REPORT
Baby's death probed as homicide

Inquest possible in infant's death

The police determined the child had been tossed across a creek where she landed with such impact on the frozen ground and hard packed snow that it caused injury to the baby's chest area resulting in the internal bleeding.

The body of the child was covered with a fresh layer of snow indicating the baby had been left outside for a considerable amount of time. The autopsy revealed baby Nicole died clutching a single blade of grass in her tiny hand, she was alive as she laid in the backyard of her grandparents house, bleeding internally from being so callously thrown onto the snow covered ground. The child was left by her killer to freeze to death.

When details of the brutal death of the innocent 10-month-old child became known the public was outraged. People wanted to know how someone could throw an infant onto the cold hard ground and leave the helpless child there to freeze to death? What kind of heinous fiend was living in their community? Were other children safe from the maniac who killed baby Nicole Hattamer?

The police initially suspected the baby's father or one of the child's relatives in the home was responsible for the murder of tiny baby Nicole. But, there was not enough evidence for the prosecutor to lay charges against anyone.

A closed door hearing was held in 1990 and another in 1998 where several witnesses were called but according to the prosecutor nothing new came from the hearings.

DNA or other advancements in forensic technology have not helped the authorities in finding the killer of baby Nicole. Two dozen years after the death of Nicole the case is still an active murder investigation that is reviewed periodically, but no new evidence has been found.

If readers have any information that could assist in bringing the murderer of 10-month-old Nicole Lee Hattamer to justice, they should contact Lake Holcombe Police Department.

If I Am Found Murdered, Find My Killer And See That Justice Is Done

On September 2, 1974, the three Reker sisters, Mary 15, Susan, 12, and Elizabeth, 13 wanted to walk to a shopping center not far from their house. They needed to pick up a few school supplies. But at the last minute, Elizabeth decided to stay at home and help her mother around the house.

About 11:00 AM, while the girls father painted the exterior of the family house, he waved to two of his daughters as they walked away.

Mrs. Reker was busy around the house and lost track of time. When she noticed it was after 5:00 PM and the girls had not returned yet she was angry, and concerned. The girls knew better than to stay away so long.

As the afternoon became evening, Mrs. Reker made calls to neighbors and the girl's friends, possibly they had met some friends and gone to one of their houses. Mr. Reker and their son rode around the neighborhood looking for the girls. The girls were not located.

Fifteen year old Mary, left and twelve year old Susan Reker.

Great Lakes Cold Case Files..

That evening the Reker's went to the St. Cloud, Minnesota police department to ask if they had any information about the missing girls.

St. Cloud man asks help in search for missing daughters

The parents were surprised and insulted by the reaction they received from the police. The police treated the missing girls as runaways. They told the parents they usually wait 48 hours before spending much time investigating because most of the time kids ran away and returned within that time span.

They tried to explain that the girls were not the type to run away. They did not have a shattered home life they were running from, they were not abused children, and they had no reason to run away from home.

The police accepted that the two teenagers were not runaways and began a missing person investigation. The girl's description was printed in area newspapers and posted around the area.

Mary, 15, was 5'-3" tall, 115 pounds with greenish eyes, brown hair and she wore gray wire rim glasses. When she left the house she was wearing blue jeans, and an army shirt with "Reker" printed on the front.

Twelve-year-old Susan was 4'-11" in height, 100 pounds, had waist length dark brown hair and wore gold wire rim glasses. She was wearing a white cotton short jacket and blue corduroy pants when she left the house with her sister.

The police interviewed employees at the store where the girls told their mother they wanted to go. They remembered the two teenagers shopping about 1:30. The girls had made it to the store and must have disappeared after shopping or on their way home.

As the hours turned to days, the authorities, family and friends mounted an intensive search of the area. Unfortunately, their efforts were met with failure. The girls were not heard from or seen again.

On September 28, 1974 a grizzly discovery was made at a water filled stone quarry three miles outside St. Cloud where area teens gathered. Hidden in tall weeds, Susan's dead body was found. She had been stabbed 13 times.

The area was searched for Mary, but no evidence or signs of the second missing girl were found. A team of divers were brought in to search the quarry. Forty feet below the surface, they found Mary's body. She was unclothed and had been stabbed six times.

... If I Am Found Murdered, Find My Killer And See That Justice Is Done

With the location of the bodies being outside the city of St. Cloud, the double murder became the jurisdiction of the Stearns County Sheriff's Department.

That the bodies were found at the quarry where area teens gathered on warm summer days, led investigators to believe the person or persons responsible for the deaths of the two girls was someone familiar with the area. Was there a heinous murderer living amongst them?

Tips flooded in to the sheriff's office and were followed up, but no suspects were found. Psychics and mediums came forward to tell the deputies of visions they had that might help them find the murderer of the teenagers but none proved to be viable.

One strange discovery was made on the back page of Mary Reker's diary. In Mary's handwriting it was written; "If I am found murdered, find my killer and see that justice is done."

The family or her friends could not give an explanation as to why 15 year old Mary would think and write such a prophetic statement.

Also in the diary was found a list of people whom she wanted to have pieces of her stuffed animal collection in the event of her death.

The investigation continued but as the months became years, hope that whomever had so viciously stabbed the two young girls would be discovered and brought to justice dwindled. Years grew to decades and no one was arrested in the murder of the Reker girls. However the Sheriff's department was very interested in one man who lived just a few blocks from the Reker family; Michael Bartowsheski.

Three years after the Reker girls were brutally stabbed to death another young girl, Michelle Talbott, was stabbed and slashed to death in Colorado. The man found guilty of the crime was Michael Bartowsheski.

Bartowsheski explained that when he killed the Colorado girl he was so drunk and full of rage that he could not control himself. Even if he wanted to stop thrusting his knife into the girl he could not.

"I was out of my mind." He said in a prison interview.

The Reker girls and the Colorado youth were both stabbed repeatedly in the chest. Michelle Talbott's neck was also slashed. The type of knife Bartowsheski used in the murder of Michelle Talbott was the same type used to murder Mary and Susan Reker.

The knife was also the same type identified to have been used in the abduction and attempted murder of Bev Servio in St. Cloud, Minnesota two years after the Reker girls were found murdered.

Servio and her infant child were kidnapped by a man and ordered to drive her car while the kidnapper sat in the front passenger seat. She intentionally drove off the road, came to a stop, grabbed her child and ran from the car.

Michael Bartowsheski was charged with four felonies in the Servio case.

Bartowsheski claimed he committed the horrific crimes when he was so drunk he could not remember doing so. Despite this, he adamantly states he could not have killed Mary and Susan Reker because at the time of their deaths he was only 15 years old and did not drink at that age.

While Michael Bartowsheski has been questioned numerous times and remains a person of interest in the gruesome murder of the teenage sisters from St. Cloud, Minnesota he has never been arrested for the crime.

The authorities have another man they are interested in talking to about the deaths of the Reker girls. The man has served prison time for a crime involving another Minnesota girl. They have not disclosed the man's name as of yet but they continue to investigate his possible involvement in the murders.

Some intriguing similarities exist between the crime the second suspect served time for and the deaths of the Reker teens; Mary Reker and the victim in the second case were approximately the same age and were stabbed with similar small knives. In both cases the girls blouses or sweaters were sliced up the middle. In each case the girls bras and panties were cut and removed. In both cases the girl's undergarments were tossed in a lake. The Reker girls bodies were hidden, one in tall weeds and the other in the quarry and in the second case the victim was covered with branches and leaves.

Despite all of the intriguing similarities between the second suspect and Michael Bartowsheski and the death of the Reker girls, no one has been arrested in the murder of Mary and Susan Reker. The case remains an active case investigated by the Stearns County Sheriff's Department.

If anyone has information that can help identify the killer of the two innocent teenage girls, Mary and Susan Reker, they are asked to please contact the Stearns County Sheriff's Department.

Unsolved Homicides

Hundreds of crimes and murders go unsolved throughout the Great Lakes region and nationwide thousands of murders are not solved. Many large cities and most states and Canadian provinces have developed Internet websites devoted to asking for help from its citizens in solving crimes. The following information is just a brief example of Great Lakes region websites dedicated to seeking information to solve crimes. For a more in-depth study of unsolved crime, visit the sites listed in the bibliography of this text or perform an Internet search. Help bring closure to the families of the deceased.

Illinois Unsolved Homicides

The following are just a small portion of the unsolved homicides that took place in Illinois. To find more information about unsolved murders in Illinois, an internet search will reveal several sites about unsolved homicides where the authorities are reaching out to the public.

Tamoi Taylor

On December 16, 1983, a fourth grade student at St. Catherine – St. Lucy Catholic School in Oak Park, Illinois, Tamoi Taylor began walking home along a route she and her mother had discussed when school was dismissed early.

A friend of Tamoi's called her to make sure she had gotten home but Tamoi's mother did not know that students were released early so she set out to meet Tamoi along the route her daughter was to take. She did not find her Tamoi.

Not finding her daughter she called the police and a search began for the missing eight year-old girl.

Later the same day the body of a young black girl was found on the side of the road in the 2000 block of West Kinzie. It was Tamoi Taylor. She was the victim of homicide.

Anyone with information that can help solve the terrible murder of a young innocent girl needs to call the Chicago Police Department, Cold Case Squad at 312-746-9690.

Jamie Santos

Jamie Santos

The Wheeling, Illinois police department received a 911 call at 11:35 AM from an unidentified man telling them that a woman was in need of medical attention.

An ambulance was rushed to the address given and the emergency medical technicians found 27-year-old Jamie Santos dead. On that day, October 28, 1991, Jamie's death was ruled a homicide.

Despite an intensive investigation by the Wheeling Police Department the man who made the 911 call has not been identified. The police do not know if the man is responsible for Jamie's death or a good samaritan.

Anyone with information that could lead to the identity of the 911 caller and or information as to who killed Jamie Santos are asked to call the Wheeling Police Department at 847-459-2632.

Carol Rofstad

On December 23, 1975, a pretty 21-year-old Illinois State University student was bludgeoned unconscious outside her sorority house in Normal, Illinois. An 18-inch long section of railroad tie found nearby was determined to be the weapon used. The next day, Carol Rofstad died from her injuries.

There were no witnesses to the murder, but some witnesses told police of two men they had seen in the area of the soror-

21 year old Carol Rofstad.

ity house the day before. The police made a sketch of one of the suspects based on the witness's observation.

In the nearly 40 years that have passed since the violent death of Carol Rofstad, her murderer has not been brought to justice. If anyone has any information that will aid the Normal, Illinois police in this cold case murder should call 309-454-9526.

A sketch of a person the police are interested in talking with about the murder of Carol Rofstad.

Unidentified Female

A digital image of the unidentified woman.

On July 20, 1990, a white female body was found in a field about 40 feet north of Lebanon Road in Collinsville, Illinois. The female was between 5'-4" and 5'-6" tall and 120 to 130 pounds. The victim had been slashed and stabbed in the neck and torso. She was also mutilated; her fallopian tubes, uterus and ovaries had been removed from the body.

The identity of the victim nor that of the murderer has not been established. Anyone with information should call the Madison County Sheriff's office at 618 692-4433.

Lorraine F. Bieze

On August 3, 1982, twenty one year old Lorraine Bieze was found near the Chicago Central and Pacific railroad tracks, not far from the Pratt's Wayne Woods Forest Preserve in Wayne Township. An autopsy showed Lorraine had been sexually assaulted, then strangled.

The murder of Lorraine Bieze remains unsolved if anyone has information that will help bring her killer to justice are asked to call the Illinois State Police at 815-224-1171.

Lorraine Bieze was raped and strangled.

Tammy J. Zywicki

Tammy Zywicki, murdered on her way to college.

Tammy Zywicki left her house in Evanston, Illinois on August 23, 1992 heading to college in Grinnell, Iowa. Later the same day, an Illinois State Trooper ticketed her car for being an abandoned car on the side of the highway. The next day, following protocol, the State Police towed the car to an impound lot.

Tammy's mother called the police to report her daughter had left home but never showed up at her destination. A missing person investigation began and on September 1, 1992 Tammy Zywicki's body was found along I-44 in rural Lawrence County, between Springfield and Joplin, Missouri. Tammy had been stabbed to death.

Witnesses reported seeing Tammy's car on I-80 at mile marker 83 in LaSalle County, Illinois. They also stated seeing a semi-truck and trailer near her car with a driver described as a white male over six feet tall and between 35 and 40 years old.

Missing from Tammy's belongings are a Canon 35 MM camera and a watch with an umbrella on the face and the watch played a musical tune.

Anyone with information about the murder of Tammy Zywicki needs to contact the Illinois State Police at 815-224-1171.

John Pate

Mr. Pate was employed as a security guard at a group of federal buildings in the South Loop of Chicago, Illinois. On occasion he went to the taverns in the area after his shift ended at 1:00 AM. He was last seen in a bar on South State Street on May 26, 1998. His body was found the next day around the 900 block of LaSalle Street, at the time an area used for overflow parking.

Near his body was a commercial vehicle that had been stolen. Mr. Pate's car was found that morning in North Chicago and the car had been intentionally set afire.

Anyone with information that can help lead to the apprehension of the murderer of John Pate should call the Chicago Police Department, Cold Case Squad at 312-746-9690.

Michigan Unsolved Homicides

The following are a random sampling of unsolved homicides that have occurred in Michigan. If anyone has any information about any of these unsolved cases found on the internet, they are encouraged to call the local police department, the sheriff's office or the Michigan State Police.

Christopher Fandel

On October 5, 2011, Lansing, Michigan Police responded to a 911 call at 9:00 PM about gunshots being fired at the intersection of Chestnut and Hillsdale within the city.

The officers discovered a car parked near the intersection with Christopher Fandel seated in the front seat. He had been shot several times and was dead.

A person who witnessed the murder was able to assist the police in making a composite drawing of the suspect. The Lansing Police ask that if anyone can identify the person in the sketch or has any information about the crime, call them or contact Mid Michigan Crime Stoppers at 517-483-STOP.

A police sketch of the man wanted for questioning in the murder of Christopher Fandel.

Donna Gomez

Donna Potas Gomez was murdered in her house in Lincoln Park, Michigan.

The community of Lincoln Park, located downriver from Detroit was shocked by a murder of one of its residents. On August 2, 1985, the police were called to the home of Donna Gomez. Donna was found dead.

Donna, a 1980 graduate of Lincoln Park High School, worked three jobs including being a track coach at her alma mater.

Sometime between 10:30 PM on August 1st and 5:30 AM on August 2, a person or persons entered the Gomez home on Cleveland Street while Donna was home and her husband Danny away. The perpetrators murdered Donna and escaped unnoticed.

Donna Gomez's murder has not been solved and anyone with information that might help the police identify the killers is asked to call the Lincoln Park Police. There is a reward available for the arrest and conviction of Donna Gomez's murderer.

Kiontae Atkins

On August 8, 2011 at about 5:00 PM, gunshots rang out on the streets of Detroit. On the 8200 block of Carlin, a car drove down the street and someone opened fire on persons on the street. Thirty four year old Kiontae Atkins, standing outside his mother's house, was shot and died from his wounds. He was not the intended target; he was an innocent bystander. Anyone with information in the murder of Kiontae is asked to call the Detroit Police. A reward is being offered.

Kiontae Atkins an innocent victim of a drive by shooting.

Michael James Roy

Michael and another man drove to a friend of Michael's house, on the 800 block of Green Road in the city of Ypsilanti, Michigan. Around 12:15 AM on January 5, 2009, the person whom Michael brought to the house produced a gun and attempted to rob the residence of the house of money and drugs.

Michael tried to intercede and stop the robbery and was shot and killed for his efforts. The murderer ran from the house before police arrived.

Michael Roy was a victim of a friend.

The residents of the house had never seen the man before and could not provide his name, but described the unidentified man, as a light skinned black man, approximately 25-30 years old, between 5'-4" and 5'-7" tall. He was wearing a t-shirt and Carhartt® hooded jacket.

A reward is being offered for the arrest and conviction of the man who murdered Michael James Roy. Any information that can assist in apprehending the murderer should call the Ypsilanti Police.

James Russel Honeycutt

On December 19, 2005, thirty-year-old James Honeycutt was shot in the back during an apparent robbery. His body was found in the 300 block of Second Street in Jackson, Michigan. The victim's pockets had been searched for anything valuable.

The suspect in the killing, described as a black male wearing a black puffy winter coat, standing between 6'-0" and 6'-2" and weighing 200 to 220 pounds was last seen running west on Washington Street.

Anyone with information that can help the police bring the murderer of James Russell Honeycutt to justice should call the Jackson Police Department.

James Honeycutt, the victim of a robbery gone tragically wrong.

George Johnson

Over twenty years ago, on September 2, 1993, a blue four-door Cadillac was found in Tuscola County in the western Thumb of Michigan's lower peninsula. In the trunk of the car, the Tuscola Sheriff's Department discovered the body of George Johnson.

Johnson was last seen earlier that day working around his house on South Warren Street in the city of Saginaw.

Who murdered George Johnson?

It was reported to the authorities that Johnson was having some trouble with some people from his area. Could his death be related?

Anyone with information that can help the Michigan State Police find the person responsible for the death of George Johnson should contact the MSP at 517-204-0808.

Ohio Unsolved Homicides

The following is a sampling of unsolved murders that occurred in the state of Ohio. The information is from the Ohio Attorney General website. If anyone has information about these or any unsolved homicides in Ohio, should contact their local police, Sheriff's Department or the Ohio Bureau of Criminal Investigation.

Bobby Ann Waymire

The body of Bobby Ann Waymire was found in Clark County, Ohio on October 23, 1972. The 5'-4", 110 pound brunette had been strangled and the body dumped along the side of Haddix Road, 1.25 miles west of State Route 444.

This is an open case and if anyone has information on the murder of Bobby Ann Waymire they should call the Clark County Sheriff's office at 937-328-2560.

Harun L. Frizzell

On August 20, 2011, Harun and a female friend were sitting on his 1989 Chevrolet Blazer on 4108 East 147th Street, Cleveland, Ohio when a 5'-2" black male, in a gray hoodie, wearing black knee length shorts and holding a gun in each hand ordered them to the ground and demanded money. The 238 pound, 6'-1" Frizzell told him he had no money. The 135 pound suspect then demanded the keys to Frizzell's vehicle. The two men began to fight and during the struggle the suspect discharged his gun shooting Frizzell in the head, then drove off in the Blazer. No one has been arrested in the death of Harun Frizzell. Anyone with knowledge of the crime should contact the Cleveland Police, Homicide Unit.

Great Lakes Cold Case Files..

Angela Marie Steele

On June 4, 1999, Michael Steele called 911 at 7:11 AM informing police that his wife's car was burned in a car accident. When Wyandotte County Sheriff's Deputies arrived at the rural location in Marseilles Township, they found a car belonging to Steele's wife that had crashed into a tree a short distance from their home. Five foot eight inch, 130 pound Angela Marie Steele was found dead in the front seat of the car. Due to the intense fire, an autopsy performed on her body did not reveal the cause of her death but the fire was discovered to be arson and her death a homicide. The Sheriff's investigation established the automobile accident had been staged to try to cover the murder of the blonde hair, blue-eyed woman. Despite an extensive investigation, the person or persons who murdered the thirty-year-old woman remain free.

If anyone has information that would lead to the arrest and conviction of the murderer should contact the Wyandotte County Sheriff's Department at 414-294-2362.

James K. Skulka

On August 13, 1998, Jim Skulka, a 36 year old, 6'-0", 170 pound male was last seen leaving his job at Coopers Electronics in Mount Vernon, Ohio not to be seen alive again. Nine days later, Coshocton County Sheriff's Deputies found Skulka's car off Highway 57 in Bedford Township. Upon examining the automobile, they discovered James Skulka in the trunk of the vehicle. He had been shot in the head.

The case of James Skulka remains open, nobody has been convicted his murder. Anyone with information about the murder of James Skulka should contact the Coshocton County Sheriff's Department or the Ohio Bureau of Criminal Investigation at 330-659-4707.

Rayshon Jamaar Thomas

On September 5, 1998, Rayshon, aka Shawn, was at 15600 Terrace Road, Apartment 1103, East Cleveland, Ohio with a few others. An unknown black male entered the apartment, tied up the occupants and demanded money. Shawn, 5'-7" and 160 pounds, was able to free himself and struggled with the thief. In the struggle, the unknown male shot three times striking Rayshon twice.

Anyone with knowledge of the unknown black male who shot and killed Rayshon Thomas should contact the Ohio Bureau of Criminal Investigation at 330-659-4707.

Margaret Cecelia Durant

Petite, 5'-3", 101 pound, 21 year old Margaret Durant was found dead on December 11, 1987 in a vacant lot near the intersection of Burrell and Higgs Avenues in Grandview Heights, Ohio, in Franklin County. She had been last seen leaving the Limited Distribution Center on Morris Road in Columbus, Ohio. Margaret died of strangulation.

If anyone has information that can assist in the capture of the murderer of Margaret Durant are asked to call the Grandview Heights Police Department at 614-488-7901.

Minnesota Unsolved Homicides

Unsolved murders exist in all of the United States; Michigan, Illinois, Ohio, Indiana, Wisconsin, Pennsylvania, New York and Minnesota and the Canadian Province of Ontario make up the Great Lakes Region. The following are some unsolved homicides that have occurred in Minnesota.

Cynthia Haisley

Forty three year old Cynthia Haisley was homeless and living beneath a bridge in northwest Rochester, Minnesota. It is thought she lived with several other homeless. Cynthia took advantage of private and public assistance for the homeless such as the Day Care Center and the Salvation Army in Rochester.

Cynthia Haisley

On October 3, 1998, Cynthia's body was found beneath the bridge. She had been beaten to death.

Anyone who has information that can assist the police to solve this murder of Cynthia Haisley is asked to contact the Rochester Police Department at 507-328-6888 or the Minnesota Bureau of Criminal Apprehension, Cold Case Homicide Unit at 888-234-3692.

A reward of up to $20,000 is being offered.

Frank Kastelic, a victim of an unknown killer.

Frank Kastelic

On April 18, 1989, Frank Kastelic, 52 years old, who taught in an elementary school and also was a part time U.S. Customs Inspector in the St. Paul, Minnesota area died from a single gunshot wound.

At approximately 6:00 in the morning, a vehicle bumped into Mr. Kastelic's car at the intersection of Stillwater Road and Algonquin Street in St. Paul. When he got out of his car, the person who bumped into the Kastelic car pulled out a gun and shot him in the head.

A witness to the incident described the murderer as a man approximately 20 to 25 years old, stocky build with long black hair. His facial features indicated he may be a Native American. The car he was driving was described as possibly a 1973 orange Chevrolet Laguna.

Great Lakes Cold Case Files

If anyone has knowledge that can assist in solving this cold case that are asked to call St. Paul Police Department, Homicide Unit at 651-266-5650.

Kevin Brewer

On August 3, 2000 about 10:00 PM, eleven year old Kevin Brewer was walking with a friend near Cottage Park in North Minneapolis when they saw a fight breakout between men who were gambling on the street. There were about one hundred people present watching the altercation when gunshots rang out and Kevin was hit three times.

Since 2000 no one has been arrested in the death of the innocent eleven-year-old bystander. If anyone has any information in the death of Kevin Brewer that are asked to contact the Minneapolis Police Department at 612-673-2358, or the Minnesota Bureau of Criminal Apprehension, Cold case Homicide Unit at 615-793-7000.

Jacques Dortch

Eighteen year old Jacques was sitting in a car near home on October 25, 2008 when an unidentified man walked up to the car and started shooting a gun into the interior of the car. Jacques and another person were shot. Jacques died from wounds in the unprovoked shooting.

The killer of Jacques Dortch has not been identified. The St. Paul Police Department is asking for help in the case of the murder of Jacques Dortch. They ask that people with information contact the Crime Stoppers of Minnesota Hotline at 800-222-8477.

Cindy Joy Elias

Its going on almost 40 years since Cindy Elias was beaten so severely about the head that she died, but her murderer still walks free. Cindy's body was found on the morning of March 24, 1977 off a logging road north of Aurora, Minnesota. She had been buried beneath a pile of brush.

Nineteen-year-old Cindy was last seen at 12:30 AM in a bar in Virginia, Minnesota where she was looking for a ride home and said she was going to hitchhike.

The authorities theorize that the person or persons who murdered Cindy Elias might be local and familiar with the area where Cindy's body was found.

Any information that helps bring closure to Cindy's family should call the St. Louis Sheriff's Department or the Tip Line at 877-996-6222.

Wisconsin Unsolved Homicides

The following are examples of homicides that occurred in Wisconsin. An internet search will reveal many more murders where the authorities have reached out to the public for assistance.

James Southworth

On November 23, 2001, 37-year-old James Southworth was hunting on a relative's property outside of Chili, Wisconsin, near the center of the state. Around 7:30 the next morning, the body of Mr. Southworth was found. He had been shot in the back twice.

It was raining and any fingerprints or footprints had been washed away.

Witnesses told authorities on the day of the shooting they saw a late 1980s silver, gray or off white Nissan or Chevy S-10 pick-up truck parked on a road near where James' body was found. The truck had a tan, beige or off white stripe on the sides low to the ground. The witnesses also described three Asian men they saw standing around the pick-up. The police would like to talk to the three individuals; possibly they may have witnessed something.

The murder of James Southworth remains unsolved to this day. Anyone with information to assist in solving the killing of Southworth are asked to call the Division of Criminal Investigation at 715-839-3830, or the Clark County Sheriff's Department at 800-743-2420. The family and friends of James Southworth have established a $50,000 reward for information leading to the arrest and conviction of those responsible for the death of James Southworth.

Barbara F. Blackstone

On August 5, 1987, two hunters walking the woods near Paulson Road in Lafayette County found the body of Barbara Blackstone. An autopsy revealed that she was a victim of a homicide. The thirty year old Ms. Blackstone had been missing since July 9, 1987 when she was seen at Scully's International Shell gas station. During their investigation, the police determined that she disappeared from her home on Delmore Road in Juneau County.

The authorities request anyone with information on this cold case to contact the Division of Criminal Investigation at 608-266-1671, or contact the Lafayette County Sheriffs Department at 608-776-4870 or the Juneau County Sheriff's Department directly at 608-847-5649.

Terry L. Smith

On August 28, 1981, Terry Smith and his wife drove to Wisconsin Dells, approximately 50 miles north of the state's capitol in Madison. His wife reported dropping him off downtown after they had spent time in the Two G's Bar. Terry was going to stay with family in the area.

Terry disappeared and was not seen again until November 28, 1981, two months later, when two hunters came across his partially decomposed body. An autopsy showed that Terry Smith had died as the result of a gunshot to his chest.

Terry's death has yet to be solved. Anyone with information that can help the authorities bring Terry Smith's murderer to justice should call the Division of Criminal Investigation at 608-266-1671, or contact the Adams County Sheriff's Department directly at 608-339-3304.

"Joe Doe"

On September 21, 1982, a logging crew was working on private property in Barron County, Wisconsin, when they made a gruesome discovery, a human skeleton.

They found the remains of a man, the pathologist describes as, between 18 and 22 years old, weighing between 180 and 195 pounds, 5'-8" to 5'-9", with a husky build and brown hair. Despite the remains being skeletal with very little soft tissue, the pathologists determined the man had been stabbed three times with a knife with a blade long enough to penetrate through the chest and leave serrations on the spine. Joe Doe had been murdered.

The authorities tried to make identification by dental records but no dental records of missing persons matched the dental impressions taken from Joe Doe.

The skeleton found in the woods of Wisconsin had a surgically repaired broken leg. The repairs included a staple in the bone, several stainless steel screws, and a pin in the leg. The surgical pin was imprinted with a serial number but the deputies working the case were still not able to make identification.

In 2000, a facial reconstruction specialist was brought in to make a clay model of what Joe Doe may have looked like. The process adds clay to represent flesh to the skull in known thickness, rendering an approximate image of what the victim looked like at the time of his death. Despite the reconstruction process Joe Doe was not identified.

Without knowing who was killed, solving the murder case is next to impossible.

Three decades after Joe Doe was found in a northwestern Wisconsin woods, his identity and his murderer remain unknown. Any information about this unsolved case should be reported to the Barron County Sheriff's Department at 715-537-3106.

Bibliography

I Am A Cheat But Not A Murderer

Traverse City Record-Eagle, Traverse City, Michigan, July 23, 24, 25, 1968.

Traverse City Record-Eagle, Traverse City, Michigan, June 21, 2008.

Car & Driver Magazine, John Phillips, April 2012,
www.caranddriver.com/comparisons/2012-nissan-juke-sv-awd-vs-2011-mini-cooper-s-countryman-all4-2012-jeep-compass-latitude-4x4-comparison-test

A&E Community, "Robison Family Murders 1968 Good Hart, Michigan,"
www.community.aetv.com/service/displayDiscussionThreads.kickAction?w=267379&as=119137&d=332987

Wikipedia, the free encyclopedia, "Robison family murders,"
www.wikipedia.org/wiki/Robison_family_murders

Good Hart Michigan; Enchanting Good Hart of Pure Northern Michigan,
Robison Family Murders ~ 40 Years Cold,
www.ballybowler.wordpress.com/2008/07/11/robison-murders-are-40-years-cold/

The Ludington Daily News, Ludington, Michigan, January 7, 13, 1970.

Great Lakes Cold Case Files..

I Want To Be A Priest

"12 years later: the Father Alfred Kunz (unsolved) murder," March 3, 2010, Matt C. Abbott,

www.renewamerica.com/columns/abbott/100303

Lodi Valley News, Lodi, WI, March 6, 2009, Lou Holt,

"Who Killed Father Kunz?" www.lodivalleynews.com/local/murder-at-st-michaels/

Cover story, The Devil And Father Kunz, "An Easter tale about murder, the Catholic Church and the strange paths of good and evil," Chuck Nowlen, April 12, 2001, Las Vegas Weekly/Radiant City Publications, www.chuck-knowlen.com/kunz.htm

Got Questions.com, The Bible has answers, What is Luciferianism?, www.gotquestions.org/Luciferianism.html

Wisconsin State Journal, Madison, Wisconsin, March 5, 6, 1998.

Who Killed The Boy In The Box?

Chester Times, Chester, Pennsylvania, February 27, 1957.

The Daily Courier, Connellsville, Pennsylvania, February 28, 1957.

Delaware County Daily Times, Chester, Pennsylvania, November 9, 1962.

Lebanon Daily News, Lebanon, Pennsylvania, March 2, 1957.

Front Page Detective Magazine, "Who is the boy in the box?," November, 1957.

Saturday Evening Post, A Box, A Blanket, and a Small Body," July 1957.

A Brutal Beating In A Rural Setting

Delayed Justice, Sidney P. Hildebrant, www.delayedjustice.com/?p=4480

Why Didn't They Leave My Babies Alone?

Mt Vernon Register News, Mt Vernon, Illinois, Wednesday, August 21, 1957

Mt Vernon Register News, Mt Vernon, Illinois, Friday, May 24, 1957

Southtown Economist, Chicago, Illinois, Wednesday, January 23, 1957

The Daily Register, Harrisburg, Illinois, Tuesday, November 01, 1955

Dixon Evening Telegraph, Dixon, Illinois, Monday, November 14, 1955

The Edwardsville Intelligencer, Edwardsville, Illinois, Wednesday, October 19, 1955

Freeport Journal-Standard, Freeport, Illinois, Thursday, January 31, 1957

Southtown Economist, Chicago, Illinois, Wednesday, January 23, 1957

Reader; News and Politics, Death and the Maidens, www.chicagoreader.com/chicago/death-and-the-maidens/Content?oid=892961

Wikipedia, Murder of the Grimes Sisters, www.wikipedia.org/wiki/Murder_of_the_Grimes_sisters

Weird and Haunted Chicago, The Schueesler – Robinson Murders, www.prairieghosts.com/spmurders.html

Great Lakes Cold Case Files..

A Parents Worst Nightmare

Cold Serial... Cold Unsolved, Serial, Homicide Cases, "Oakland County Child Killings" www.michigandoes.com/ColdSerial/occk.html

Bonnie's Blog of Crime, Unsolved Serial Killings: Oakland County Child Murders "The Babysitter," www.mylifeofcrime.wordpress.com/2012/02/08/unsolved-serial-killings-oakland-county-child-murders-the-babysitter/

The Girl from the Ghetto, Was Christopher Busch The Oakland County Child Killer?, www.thegirlfromtheghetto.wordpress.com/2010/12/28/christopher-busch-the-oakland-county-child-killer/

From Wikipedia, the free encyclopedia, "Oakland County Child Killer," www.wikipedia.org/wiki/Oakland_County_Child_Killer

Herald-Palladium, Benton Harbor, Michigan, December 28, 1976.

Herald-Palladium, Benton Harbor, Michigan, March 23, 24, 1977.

Ludington Daily News - Friday, February 20, 1976, Ludington, Michigan

I Think They Have Killed Marilyn

Albuquerque Journal, Albuquerque, New Mexico, May 3, 1964.

Chronicle Telegram, Elyria, Ohio, July 15, 1954, October, 20, 1954, November 16, 1954, December 29, 1954.

Evening Independent, Massillon, Ohio, July 21, 23, 1954.

Famous Trials, "Dr. Sam Sheppard Trials," www.law2.umkc.edu/faculty/projects/ftrials/sheppard/samsheppardtrial.html

The Sam Sheppard Case, by Allison Haber, Renu Kapur, Brian Perry, and Jason Schwartz, www.bsos.umd.edu/gvpt/gvpt339/sheppard.html

Sandusky Register Star News, Sandusky, Ohio, July 21, 1954.

Sandusky Register Star News, Sandusky, Ohio, December 16, 1954.

The Times Recorder, Zaneville, OH, December 2, 1954.

Who Shot Michael Lovejoy?

The Brantford Police Service, www.brantfordpolice.ca/cold-case-files/michael-lovejoy

The Handsome Doctor And The Beautiful Widow

Lakeshore Guardian, Countryside Yarns, The Sparling Murders parts 1 & 2, Janis Stein, February, March, April, May, June, 2008.

Huron Daily Tribune, New Novel re-examines 100-year old murder mysteries, August 29, 2008.

Huron Daily Tribune, December 1,15, 22, 1911

Huron Daily Tribune, April 5, 12, 19, 26, 1912.

Huron Daily Tribune, May 3, 10, 17, 24, 31, 1912.

Huron Daily Tribune, January 5, 12, 19, 26, 1912

Huron Daily Tribune, February 2, 1912

Huron Daily Tribune, June 7, 14, 1912

Huron Daily Tribune, July 12, 19

Its Not A Job, It Becomes An Obsession

Capital Times, Madison, Wisconsin, Monday, May 27, 1968

Capital Times, Madison, Wisconsin, Wednesday, June 26, 1968

Great Lakes Cold Case Files..

Crime Library; Criminal minds and methods, Capital City Murders, David Lohr,
www.trutv.com/library/crime/serial_killers/unsolved/madison_wi/2.html

The Daily Tribune, Wisconsin Rapids, Wisconsin, Thursday, January 02, 1975

Fond Du Lac Commonwealth Reporter, Fond Du Lac, Wisconsin, Friday, July 05, 1968

Herald Times Reporter, Manitowoc, Wisconsin, Tuesday, October 12, 1976

Wisconsin State Journal, Madison, Wisconsin, Friday, March 05, 1982

Wisconsin State Journal, Madison, Wisconsin, Saturday, May 02, 1981

Wisconsin State Journal, Madison, Wisconsin, Sunday, May 28, 1972

Wisconsin State Journal, Madison, Wisconsin, Tuesday, January 13, 1976

Wisconsin State Journal, Madison, Wisconsin, Friday, March 05, 1982

Julie Speerschneider Murder – Unsolved,
www.surroundedbyreality.com/Misc/Crimes/JulieS.asp

The Bombing of Sterling Hall (The Antiwar Movement in the USA thirty four years ago today)

LeeMark Communications ^ I 2000 I Christopher J. Lee, www.freerepublic.com/focus/f-news/1198045/posts

The Death Of Sharin' Morningstar Keenan

CBC.CA, Casefile, "The Murder of Sharin' Morningstar Keenan," www.cbc.ca/news/coldcase/cases/morningstar-keenan.html

Experience Project, "Her Name Was Sharin' Morningstar Keenan," www.experienceproject.com/stories/Made-A-Promise-I-Couldnt-Keep/471886

Toronto Police, Homicide Squad, Most Wanted, "Victim: Sharin' Morningstar Keenan." www.torontopolice.on.ca/homicide/case/21

Cyanide Will Kill You

CNN Justice, FBI: We want Unabomber's DNA in 1982 Tylenol® case, May 19, 2011, www.articles.cnn.com/2011-05-19/justice/unabomber.tylenol_1_dna-sample_dna-issue-fni-office?_PM:CRIME

Daily Herald, Chicago, Illinois, October 2, 4, 5, 6, 8, 1982.

Daily Herald, Monday, August 15, 1983, Chicago, Illinois

Daily Republican Register, Tuesday, October 05, 1982, Mount Carmel, Illinois

Daily Republican Register, Thursday, October 28, 1982, Mount Carmel, Illinois

Daily Republican Register, Wednesday, December 15, 1982, Mount Carmel, Illinois

Daily Herald, Thursday, January 13, 1983, Chicago, Illinois

Alton Telegraph, Tuesday, October 05, 1982, Alton, Illinois

Daily Herald, Wednesday, December 29, 1982, Chicago, Illinois

A Murder Case Is Open Forever

City of Marquette, Michigan, http://www.mqtcty.org/

Cold Case Update: 10 years later. Natalie Jovonovich, August 23, 2010, www.uppermichiganssource.com/news/story.aspx?id=500714

The Marquette Mining Journal, The anatomy of a murder investigation, Marquette, Michigan, Johanna Boyle, August 21, 2009.

The Erin Taylor murder case under investigation 11 years later, Nikki Junewicz, August 23, 2010. www.uppermichiganssource.com/news/story.aspx?id=654570

Wikipedia, The Free Encyclopedia, www.wikipedia.org/wiki/-Marquette,_Michigan

Great Lakes Cold Case Files..

The Marquette Mining Journal, Marquette, Michigan, August 21, 22, 23, 24, 25, 2009

How Could Anyone Be So Cruel As To Kill My Little Girl?

The Daily News, Marshall, Michigan, November 16,17, 1905.

The Detroit News, Detroit, Michigan, March 5, 1938.

The Grand Rapids Herald, March 5,6,7,8,9,10, 1938.

The Marshall Evening Chronicle, Marshall, Michigan, March 5, 1938.

Ironwood Daily Globe, Ironwood, Michigan, March 7, 8. 1938.

JusticeDelayed.com, www.delayedjustice.com/?page_id=1935

Sabotage Of A Commercial Aircraft

AvStop.com, an online aviation magazine, "History of United Airlines," www.avstop.com.

Chicago Daily Tribune, Chicago, Illinois, October 11, 1933.

Enotes.com."United Airlines Chesterton Crash," www.enotes.com/topic/united_airlines_chesterton_crash

Nevada State Journal, Reno, Nevada, October 11, 1933.

The Star Journal, Sandusky, Ohio, October 11, 1933.

Wikipedia, the free encyclopedia, The United Airlines Chesterton Crash, www.wikipedia.org.

Who Murdered Pixie?

The Dispatch Magazine, H.J. Halterman, "The Grisly Saga of Pixie Grismore, was her murder, Twenty years ago covered up by Politics? November, 1998

Mike DeWine, Ohio Attorney General website, Ohio unsolved homicides, www.Ohioattorneygeneral.gov.

Ohio Unsolved Homicides, www.ohioattorneygeneral.gov/Enforcement/Unsolved-Cases/Cold-Case/Homicides/Grismore

The Pharos-Tribune, Logansport, Indiana, May 4, 9, 1978.

Gone And Never Seen Again

The "Hoffex Memo," Hoffa Conference, F.B.I. Headquarters, January 27, 28, 1976

www.neatorama.com/2009/07/29/what-happened-to-jimmy-hoffa/

www.newworldencyclopedia.org/entry/James_Hoffa

Mob Corner, Thom L. Jones, www.realdealmafia.com/mobcorner_hoffa.html

Neatorama, www.neatorama.com/2009/07/29/what-happened-to-jimmy-hoffa/

Reppetto, Thomas (2007). *Bringing Down the Mob: The War Against the American Mafia*. Henry Holt & Company

www.wikipedia.org/wiki/Au_Sable_River_(Michigan)#River_dams.5B11.5D

Realfoods.net "Visit to a rendering plant," www.realfoods.net/rendering-plant.html

"The Detroit Mafia, By Mario Machi," www.americanmafia.com/Cities/Detroit.html.

Great Lakes Cold Case Files..

Kelly, Robert J., *Encyclopedia of Organized Crime in the United States*. Westport, Connecticut: Greenwood Press, 2000.

Sifakis, Carl, *The Mafia Encyclopedia*, New York: Da Capo Press, 2005.

Sifakis, Carl, *The Encyclopedia of American Crime*, New York: Facts on File Inc., 2001.

Dan E. Moldea, *The Hoffa Wars*, Charter Books, New York: 1978.

Charles Brandt, *I Heard You Paint Houses: Frank "The Irishman" Sheeran and the Inside Story of the Mafia, the Teamsters, and the Last Ride of Jimmy Hoffa*, Steerforth Press, Hanover (NH, USA) 2004.

www.mafia-international.com/

"Motor City Mafia" by: Scott M Burnstein

www.detroit.cbslocal.com/2011/06/24/organized-crime-in-detroit-forgotten-but-not-gone/*

Mob Corner, Thom L. Jones, www.realdealmafia.com/mobcorner_hoffa.html

New York Magazine, "Can Playboy's Canary be Trusted?" Oct 16, 1989

Detroit Free Press, June 16, 2006

Desperate Bargain: Why Jimmy Hoffa Had to Die, Lester Velie

Dan E. Moldea, author of *The Hoffa Wars*

On July 1, 2007 *Detroit Free Press* staff writer Joel Thurtell

Hudson County Facts, Anthony Olszewski www.hudsoncountyfacts.com/hudsoncounty/?tag=thomas-andretta

With Honesty He Lived; For Honesty He Was Taken

Albion Evening Recorder, Albion, Michigan, January 12, 13, 1945.

Historical Albion Michigan, Albion history/genealogy recourses by Frank Passic, www.albionmich.com/history/histor_notebook/961215.shtml

McKay, Frank D. (1883-1965) and Hooper, Warren Green (1904-1945, Political Graveyard.com, www.politicalgraveyard.com/bio/hooper.html#761.57.67

Marshall Evening Chronicle, Marshall, Michigan, July 16, 25, 1945.

Mittenlit.com, "65 yeas ago today Michigan State Senator is Killed," www.mittenlit.com/2010/01/65-years-ago-today-michigan-state-senator-is-killed/

"Peek Through Time: Jackson brothers were prominent members of Prohibition-era Purple Gang" Leanne Smith, Jackson Citizen Patriot, January 15, 2011, www.mlive.com/living/jackson/index.ssf/2011/01/peek_through_time_jackson_brot.html

"Peek Through Time: Politician's shooting death in 1945 is still a mystery" Leanne Smith, Jackson Citizen Patriot, February 14, 2011, www.mlive.com/news/jackson/index.ssf/2011/02/peek_through_time_politicians.html

"Poster Reminder of Hooper Mystery," Frank Passic, *Albion Recorder*, Albion, Michigan, October 19, 1988

The Downfall Dictionary: Cataloging the past political scandals of the United States. www.downfalldictionary.blogspot.com/2010/08/frank-d-mckay-teflon-boss.html

The Herald Press, St. Joseph, Michigan, July 13, 16, 24, 25, 1945

The Ludington Daily News, Ludington, Michigan, July 18, 1945.

The News-Palladium, Benton Harbor, Michigan, January 23, 1945.

The State Journal, Lansing, Michigan, January 12, 13, 15, 18, 1945.

The Traverse City Record Eagle, Traverse City, Michigan, July 26, 1945.

Great Lakes Cold Case Files...

The Mad Butcher Of Kingsbury Run

Casebook: Jack the Ripper, Stephen P. Ryder and Johnno, www.casebook.org

Cleveland Memory, Kingsbury Run, www.images.ulib.csuohio.edu

Cleveland Torso Murders, "The Mad Butcher of Kingsbury Run," www.torsomurders.com

Dead Ohio, Kingsbury Run, www.deadohio.com

TruTv, The Kingsbury Run Murders or Cleveland Torso Murders, Marilyn Bardsley, www.trutv.com

The Cleveland Police Museum, Torso Murders, www.clevelandpolicemuseum.org

The Crime Library, The Cleveland Torso Murders, Elliot Ness Serial Killer Case, www.crimelibrary.com

Beatings And Murder In Toledo, Ohio

Chronicle Telegram, Elyria, Ohio, November 5, 1925.

Evening Gazette, Xenia, Ohio, October 29, 1926.

San Antonio Light, San Antonio, Texas, September 21, 1926.

Mansfield News, Mansfield, Ohio, January 20, 21, 1926.

Someone Left Baby Nicole Outside To Die

Wisconsin State Journal, Madison, Wisconsin, December 29, 1989.

Wisconsin State Journal, Madison, Wisconsin, October 18, 1990.

Wisconsin Department of Justice, Division of Criminal Investigation, www.doj.state.wi.us/dci/sa/unsolved.asp

WEAU.Com, Wisconsin's Unsolved Murders: Baby Nicole Hattamer, Feb 6, 2007, www.weau.com/home/headlines/5599661.html

If I Am Found Murdered, Find My Killer
And See That Justice Is Done

Beyond the Pine Curtain. Com, Kare11, Investigates: Reker Case, November 14, 2005. www.behindthepinecurtain.com/wordpress/kare-11-investigates-reker-case/

Daily Journal, Fergus Falls, Minnesota, September 30, 31, 1974.

Spotlight on Crime, www.spotlightoncrime.org/casehaisleycynthia.cfm

Tri-County Crime Stoppers of Minnesota, Inc., www.tricountycrimestoppers.org/specialreward/index.htm

Winona Daily News, Winona, Minnesota, September 15, 1974.

Sartell News leader Reaching Everyone, "Reker recounts nightmare of daughters' murder," www.thenewsleaders.com/reker-recounts-nightmare-of-daughters-murders

Unsolved Homicides By State
Illinois Unsolved Homicides

Illinois State Police, Unsolved Crimes, www.isp.state.il.us/crime/unsolved.cfm

DuPage Sheriff's Department, Cold Case Unit, Unsolved Murders, www.dupagesheriff.org/unsolved%20murders.htm

Chicago Police Department Central Investigations Unit, www.chicagopolice.org/COLDCASE/

Great Lakes Cold Case Files...

Michigan Unsolved Homicides

Crime Stoppers of Mid Michigan, 517-483-STOP, www.crimestopper-sofmidmichigan.com/unsolved-crimes.html

Speakup.org, www.1800speakup.org/cspublic/03_caseScroll.cfm?ct=33

Unsolved Homicides, Jackson Police Department, www.cityofjackson.org/police/unsolved-homicides

Michigan State Police, Cold Case Files, www.michigan.gov/msp/0,1607,7-123-1589_31786_55695_55696—-,00.html

Ohio Unsolved Homicides

Mike DeWine, Ohio Attorney General, Ohio Unsolved Homicides, www.ohioattorneygeneral.gov/Enforcement/Unsolved-Cases/Cold-Case

True Crime and Justice, www.karisable.com/crunsolved.htm

News Channel five on your Side, ABC, "Thousands of murders go unsolved across Ohio," www.newsnet5.com/dpp/news/local_news/investigations/thousands-of-murders-go-unsolved-across-ohio

Cleveland.com, "Crime," www.cleveland.com/coldcase/homicidedatabase/

Minnesota Unsolved Homicides

Spotlight on Crime, www.spotlightoncrime.org/case_haisley_cynthia.cfm

Tri-County Crime Stoppers of Minnesota, Inc., www.tricountycrimestoppers.org/specialreward/index.htm

St. Louis County Minnesota, Law and Public Safety, Unsolved Homicides in St. Louis County.
www.stlouiscountymn.gov/LAWPUBLICSAFETY/LawEnforcement/-UnsolvedHomicides.aspx

Wisconsin Unsolved Homicides

Wisconsin Department of Justice, Attorney General J.B. Van Hollen, www.doj.state.wi.us/dci/sa/unsolved.asp

Wisconsin Crime Rate: 1960-2010, www.disastercenter.com/crime/wicrime.htm

About The Author

Geography has played an important part in shaping Wayne "Skip" Kadar's love of the Great Lakes Region. Throughout his life he has lived in the downriver area of Detroit, Marquette, Michigan in the Upper Peninsula, Harbor Beach, Michigan in the State's "Thumb" area, and vacationed extensively in Wisconsin.

His life has taken him in many directions. He is a certified S.C.U.B.A. diver and avid boater, having owned most all types of boats from canoes to Personal Water Craft

Photo by Karen Kadar

to sailboats to a small cruiser. He is involved in lighthouse restoration, serving as the President of the Harbor Beach Lighthouse Preservation Society.

Mr. Kadar enjoys studying and researching Great Lakes maritime and true crime history and has made presentations on local, state and international levels.

An educator for thirty years, Mr. Kadar retired after 16 years as a high school principal.

In this book, Kadar explores one of his interests; true crime stories. Since attending college during the John Norman Collins murder spree, Skip has followed major crimes occurring around the Great Lakes region.

Skip lives in Harbor Beach, Michigan with his wife Karen. During the summer Skip can usually be found at the Harbor Beach Marina, on the family boat "Pirate's Lady" or at the family cottage in Manistique, Michigan.